Huîtres à la crè...

Consommé tortue.

Escalope de carrelet Mornay.

Filet m... briand.

P... ...e.

Cai... ...ade.

Asperge... ...ondue.

Glace ... de.

sa... ...chaude.

Fraises à la crème.

Café.

Published by the National Library of Australia
Canberra ACT 2600
Australia

National Library of Australia Cataloguing-
in-Publication entry

Bannerman, Colin.
   Acquired tastes: celebrating Australia's
   culinary history.

   Bibliography.
   Includes index.
   ISBN 0 642 10693 2.

   1. Cookery, Australian—History. 2. Food—
   Australia—History. 3. Food habits—Australia—
   History. I. National Library of Australia. II. Title.

641.30994

Project & manuscript editor: Paul Cliff
Designer: Beverly Swifte
Editorial assistants: Tony Twining, Lidija Pesec
NLA photographers: Henk Brusse, Loui Seselja,
Jim Nomarhas, Andrew Stawowczyk Long
Printed by: Lamb Printers, Perth

(front and back cover) Donald Friend (1914–89)
Shoppers at Night, Bondi Junction Mall
From 'Ayam-Ayam Kesayangan'
(Donald Friend Diaries: MS 5959, Item 2)
From the Manuscript Collection
(back cover) [*Girls in Kitchen Getting a Meal*] c.1900
Photograph
From the Pictorial Collection
(half-title page) George Baird Shaw (1812–83)
Still Life 1857
oil on board; 44 x 35.5 cm
(superimposed on detail of menu
shown on p. 72)
From the Pictorial Collection
National Library of Australia

acquired
TASTES
celebrating Australia's culinary history

by Colin Bannerman

with contributions by
Gay Bilson, Jackie French,
Marion Halligan and Eric Rolls

National Library of Australia
Canberra 1998

ACKNOWLEDGEMENTS

A NOTE ON THE MATERIAL

The main text of this book, with the exception of some minor additional subfeatures, was written by Colin Bannerman; supplementary features by Gay Bilson, Marion Halligan, Jackie French and Eric Rolls.

The work draws for the major part on material from the National Library of Australia's general collection, and its Pictorial, Manuscript, Oral History, Map, Ephemera and Music collections. With regard to the Oral History extracts used in the book's sidebars, for simplification these are generally indicated by means of the interviewee's initials, with date of birth given for context. Apart from those with Gay Bilson and Vern Davis, the interviews were conducted as part of the New South Wales Bicentennial Oral History Project. Fuller details are as follows. (Full names set against the initials used in the main text.)

Gay Bilson, b.1944; pp. 73, 75–76, 79, 84
Restaurateur and chef. (Recorded 1994.
Interviewed by Heather Rusden. ORAL TRC 3029)

'N.B.' Nell Brazel; pp. 51, 57
Born Arbroath, Scotland, April 1899; met Australian husband in Britain in 1917 and migrated to Australia after WWI, settling in his home town of Walcha. (Recorded 1987. Interviewed by Jenny Salmon. ORAL TRC 2301 INT.59)

'J.C.' James Castrission; pp. 58, 64
Born in Kythera, Greece, 1902; migrated to Australia in 1914; bought a café/fruit shop with his uncle in Gundagai. (Recorded 1987. Interviewed by Dimitri Rontidis. ORAL TRC 2301 INT.13)

'H.C.' Hilda Cross; pp. 15, 32, 33, 34, 36
Born at Yarrowitch near Walcha, NSW, August 1902. (Recorded 1987. Interviewed by Jenny Salmon. ORAL TRC 2301 INT.49)

'V.D.' Vern Davis; p. 35
Born southern NSW, 1928.
Stockman, cattle farmer and former dogger. (Recorded 1993. Interviewed by Chris Woodland. ORAL TRC 2976)

'A.D.' Alice Doyle; p. 44
Born 1890, Camden Haven, north coast NSW. (Recorded 1987. Interviewed by Lucy Taksa. ORAL TRC 2301 INT.124)

'G.T.' Gladys Timbs; pp. 24, 40, 41, 68, 69, 71
Born at Woollarah, Sydney's eastern suburbs, 1905. (Recorded 1987. Interviewed by Stephen Rapley. ORAL TRC 2301 INT.87)

The National Library of Australia thanks the following for reproduction of material in *Acquired Tastes*: Estate of Donald Friend (and Brown Evans & Co.); the Cazneaux family; Barbara Mobbs (literary executor for Patrick White); George Molnar; Neil James; Craig Voevodin (and University of Queensland Press); Gay Bilson, Sally Hassan and Grant Mudford; Allan Vousden; *Endeavour* Foundation. It also thanks the following publishers: Kangaroo Press (*The Art of Living in Australia*, facsimile edn, 1987); *The Australian Women's Weekly*; Greenhouse Publications (*Mrs Dorothy Floate's Secret of Success Cookery Book*); Christine Manfield (author) and Ashley Barber (photographer) and Viking/Penguin Books Australia (*Paramount Desserts*); Federal Capital Press (photograph of Simon Le Comte, p. 73); New Holland Publishers/C.J. Publishing, Michael Ryan (author), Ian Baker (photographer) (*Simply Australia: A Culinary Journey*); Penguin Books Australia (*Recipes My Mother Gave Me*); Ansay Pty Ltd (*The Naked Gourmet*; creator and author Hilary Lindsay; line drawings by Paul Delprat); Reed Books P/L (*Woman's Day Cookbook*); Text Publishing (*Eat Me*); W.H. Allen & Co. (UK) (*The Graham Kerr Cookbook*); The National Heart Foundation of Australia (*Consuming Passions: Cooking with Ian Parmenter*); The State Library of New South Wales Press (*When Mabel Laid the Table: The Folklore of Eating and Drinking in Australia*); Kangaroo Press/Simon & Schuster Aust. (*The Antipodean Cookery Book and Kitchen Companion*); HarperCollins (*Fusion: The Watermark Restaurant Cookbook*, photography by Warwick Kent); Angus & Robertson/HarperCollins (*Bush Tucker: Australia's Wild Food Harvest*). The image on p. 74 previously appeared in *Interiors* magazine, Feb. 1986. Patrick White's correspondents in his letters (extracted on pp. 61–62) are, in order: Mollie McKie, David Moore, David and Gwen Moore, Ben Huebsch, Charles Osborne, Geoffrey Dutton, Geoffrey Dutton, Ninette Dutton, James and Tania Stern, and Dorothy Green.

CONTENTS

Aberdeen and Commonwealth Line

PREFACE

F ood has become a powerful symbol of popular culture. Our attitudes towards it are deeply embedded in nearly all facets of our private and public self-consciousness. The formal Sunday lunch (known as dinner) with roast meat, pudding and relatives has long since disappeared from the Australian way of life. Yet meal times—from hasty breakfast to weekend barbecue—somehow still play a vital role in keeping families connected. Entertainment and food so often go together that images of one evoke the other: movies and popcorn, football and meat pies, and so on. Meetings of friends call for a cup of coffee, a snack or a light lunch at one of the thousands of trendy cafés and eateries that have sprung up across the country. The accelerating pace of modern living has spawned vast networks of 'fast food outlets'. A celebration of any kind without food is almost unthinkable, and what we eat or drink at it helps to define the importance of the occasion. This influence is also reflected in the torrent of cookery books which in recent years has flowed onto the market—and onto the shelves of the National Library of Australia.

For several decades historians have been zealously rewriting history: reclaiming for Australia the culture of its indigenous people, re-examining the convict records and their implications, redressing the bias that had created an overly male view of the last two centuries, filling in the gaps of social and family life left by too much concentration on public affairs and sensation. What and how Australians ate, and what they thought of it, are now coming under closer study. Much of the story, especially before about 1900, is still waiting to be told. Cookery books, fascinating as they are, provide only a small portion of the evidence needed to tell it. Much of the ephemera of the earlier period—the diaries, kitchen scrapbooks and other personal papers which can give valuable insights into the food of individuals and family groups—has unfortunately been lost. The relatively few items that have found their way into major public collections are consequently extremely valuable documents. Many other sources of information are also available to be drawn upon. Newspapers and magazines, advertising material and literary works are a useful and readily available source of data, providing their limitations are recognised. As is a vast array of related material from many other sources, such as the records of commercial interests, of contemporary researchers and regulatory bodies. The story is researched in a number of formats, from manuscript to electronic.

The National Library of Australia's wide range of material in its general and specialised holdings—its Newspaper and Microform, Oral History, Manuscript, Pictorial, and Ephemera collections—can play an important part in our understanding and appreciation of Australia's food history, both its past and the development of ongoing trends.

(opposite) Menu cover from the Aberdeen and Commonwealth Line's TSS *Esperance Bay*. The sea-fare for 7 November 1934 comprised a selection from consommé Crecy or potage Castelaine; salmon fish cakes and anchovy sauce, lamb cutlets with carrots in cream, sirloin of beef with Yorkshire pudding, or roast Surrey chicken with bread sauce, and French beans, brown and boiled potatoes; desserts were plum pudding and sweet sauce, fruit jelly, or ice cream and wafers
From the Ephemera Collection

BEGINNINGS
SEA RATIONS & DIGGING IN

I n January 1788 a motley fleet of food traditions sailed into one of the most beautiful natural harbours in the world. And when Arthur Phillip and his officers planted the British flag with all the ceremony that weary travellers could muster they also planted British food.

The bold venture to establish a colony in the antipodes had been no spur-of-the-moment decision, but the product of long and careful planning. Central to that planning was the question of how the colony was to feed itself. From all the information available, including the reports brought back by Joseph Banks and James Matra from the *Endeavour*'s earlier brief exploration of the 'new' continent, it was clear that establishing an outpost of British civilisation would be no easy task. Indigenous food cultures seem adapted to a nomadic lifestyle. There was no evidence that any local food resources could be relied upon to feed a colony that would begin with a concentrated population of a thousand people and quickly grow. The nearest trading ports were too far away and too uncertain. The best plan was to come equipped with enough food to survive for several years and with the tools, seed, plants and animals necessary to get European-style food production under way as soon as possible. In this way they would minimise the risks associated with the venture and make the best use of the knowledge and skills they already had.

Although prudence alone dictated that the new colony should bring its British food culture with it, it is unlikely that anyone on the First Fleet would have wanted much different. This was not supposed to be a gastronomic or cultural adventure; familiar food would be among the few comforts the colonists could expect—or hope for. And what they might have hoped for was the product of a motley collection of individual histories.

'FIRST CATCH YOUR HARE …'

At one extreme, the gentlemen of the Marine Corps would have brought with them some ideal of respectable British cookery. At the least, they were accustomed to 'good plain English food'—typified by the grilled chop or the beefsteak pudding. Some would have had a taste of the 'high-class' cookery of the wealthy. If any of them harboured any thoughts of remaining in the new land after their tour of duty, they probably also nurtured some hope of one day being able to dine like gentlefolk in the new land, even though many of the other comforts and amusements of polite society would be denied them.

How they might have planned to do this is not clear. Knowledge of how to make all the proper dishes—both 'high-class' and 'plain'—for a well-provided table had been built up over centuries in the great houses of Britain, and had been passed on from mistress to servant and from cook to apprentice. The proper place to learn cookery was in the kitchen.

A CHESHIRE PORK PYE FOR SEA

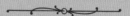

From Hannah Glasse's *The Art of Cookery Made Plain and Easy* (1747 and later), under the chapter 'For Captains of Ships'. (Another recipe in the same chapter was for 'Ketchup to Keep Twenty Years'.) This was the first time that a cookery writer had set out to provide simple and clear recipes that any competent cook could follow. As she put it in her preface:
'If I have not wrote in the high, polite Stile, I hope I shall be forgiven; for my Intention is to instruct the lower Sort, and therefore must treat them in their own Way'.

Take some salt Pork that has been boiled, cut it into thin Slices, an equal Quantity of Potatoes, pared and sliced thin, make a good Crust, cover the Dish, lay a layer of Meat, seasoned with a little Pepper, and a layer of Potatoes; then a layer of Meat, and a layer of Potatoes, and so on till your Pye is full. Season it with Pepper; when it is full, lay some butter on the Top, and fill your Dish above half full of soft Water. Close your Pye up, and bake it in a gentle Oven.

(opposite) Philip Slager (1755–1815)
View of the Part of the Town Parramatta in New South Wales, Taken from the North Side of the River 1812 (detail)
coloured engraving; 26.6 x 44 cm, plate mark
From the Pictorial Collection

1

W.B. Gould (1801–53)
Still Life c.1840
oil on canvas lined on composition board;
29.7 x 25.7 cm
From the Pictorial Collection

By the eighteenth century some very useful manuals had emerged to help those who could afford them (and whose cooks could read them). Among the popular ones were the *Compleat Housewife or Accomplish'd Gentlewoman's Companion* by Elizabeth Smith (first published 1727), and the *Experienced English Housekeeper* by Elizabeth Raffald (1769). But the most famous of them was the *Art of Cookery Made Plain and Easy*, written by 'a lady', in 1747. This work was the most advanced cookery book of its time, with clear and precise directions, and a detailed table of contents. Its recipes were divided into 22 practical chapters—with such titles as 'Of Dressing Fish', 'Of Hog's Puddings, Sausages, &c.' (which we might call *charcuterie*), 'Of Making Cakes, &c.' and 'For a Fast-Dinner, a Number of Good Dishes, Which You May Make Use of for a Table at Any Other Time'. (The number in this case was close to 300; it was the largest chapter in the book.) There was even a chapter 'For Captains of Ships', along with one headed 'A Certain Cure for the Bite of a Mad Dog' (which gave *two* cures—one for the plague, and 'how to keep clear from bugs' for good measure).

The 'lady' author was Hannah Glasse, housewife and mother of eight. Her book was an immediate success—not only with the 'lower Sort'—and remained in print for some 80 years. (Hannah Glasse's reputation lasted even longer: she entered the English language as the cook who allegedly began a recipe with the naively obvious instruction 'first catch your hare'. Nowhere, however, did she actually give such an instruction: the nearest she came was her recipe for roast hare, which began 'Take your hare when it be cas'd ...', which simply meant 'take a skinned hare'.)

JUGGED HARE

Hannah Glasse's recipe for jugged hare is a model of simplicity, yet produces a rich and aromatic stew. It was quite possibly the model for one of the finest dishes of Australian colonial cookery, the kangaroo steamer. (See p. 13.)

Cut [the hare] in little Pieces, lard them here and there with little Slips of Bacon, season them with a very little Pepper and Salt, put them into an earthen Jugg, with a Blade or two of Mace, and Onion stuck with Cloves, and a Bundle of Sweet Herbs; cover the Jugg or Jar you do it in, so close, that nothing can get in, then set it in a pot of boiling Water, keep the Water boiling, and three Hours will do it; then turn it into the Dish, and take out the Onion and Sweet Herbs, and send it to Table hot.

—Hannah Glasse, *The Art of Cookery Made Plain and Easy*

SEA-FARE

Ordinary sailors fared less well than Hannah Glasse's Cheshire Pork Pye for the Sea: their food was much more rough and ready. Ship rations were chosen rather more for their portability and convenience than for any pleasure there might have been in eating them. The basic naval ration of 1747, for example, was of salt beef, salt pork, ship's biscuit, cheese, butter, oatmeal, pease and beer. Rations on board the First Fleet were similar. The monotony of such a diet for months on end could not have encouraged sailors to care much about the finer points of food preparation. Worse—even hardy foodstuffs could deteriorate rapidly at sea, making them unpalatable or altogether unfit for consumption. (Officers often demanded that ship's biscuit be re-baked to make the weevils 'walk off'; but crew members could not afford to be so squeamish.) The high rate of disease and death among sailors, especially from scurvy, had long been a concern, but was being brought under control by the time the First Fleet set out for Botany Bay. (See *Endeavour* feature, pp. 9–11.)

At the bottom of the social ladder, convicts expected less—and generally got it—although the evidence suggests that Phillip was concerned for the welfare of the convicts under his charge and did his best to ensure that they were kept as well fed and healthy as shipboard conditions permitted.

A rather highly allegorised and romantic
rendition of the First Fleet
Thomas Gosse (1765–1844)
*Founding of the Settlement of Port Jackson
at Botany Bay in NSW* 1799
hand-coloured mezzotint; 53.8 x 60.5 cm
Rex Nan Kivell Collection; from the Pictorial Collection

Many accounts of the early years have emphasised the difficulties that faced
the First Fleet settlers immediately on their arrival at New Holland: convicts
weakened by the long sea voyage were unequal to the heavy labour now
required of them, early attempts at farming proved disappointing, and food
supplies soon ran dangerously low. For a brief period the infant colony
seemed to be on the brink of starvation. Captain Watkin Tench (*A Complete
Account of the Settlement at Port Jackson in New South Wales*, 1793) left this
record of the rations to which it was reduced after the first two years:

> Two pounds of pork, two pounds and a half of flour, two pounds of rice, or
> a quart of pease, to every grown person, and to every child of more than
> eighteen months old.

> > To every child under eighteen months old, the same
> > quantity of rice and flour, and one pound of pork.

> > (When the age of this provision is recollected, its
> > inadequacy will more strikingly appear. The pork and rice
> > were brought with us from England: the pork had been
> > salted between three and four years, and every grain of
> > rice was a moving body from the inhabitants lodged
> > within it. We soon left off boiling the pork, as it had
> > become so old and dry, that it shrunk to one half in its
> > dimensions when so dressed. Our usual method of cooking
> > it was to cut off the daily morsel, and toast it on a fork
> > before the fire, catching the drops which fell on a slice of
> > bread, or in a saucer of rice. Our flour was the remnant of
> > what was brought from the Cape, by the *Sirius*, and was
> > good. Instead of baking it, the soldiers and convicts used
> > to boil it up with greens.)

Joseph Lycett (c.1775–1828)
[*Two Aborigines beside a River Spearing Eels*; c.1817]
watercolour; 17.5 x 27.7 cm
In: *Drawings of the Natives and Scenery of Van Diemens Land*; 1820
From the Pictorial Collection

HUNTING AND GATHERING

Tench described the pathetic attempts of the settlers to catch fish and shoot kangaroos, before making the following interesting observation:

> If a lucky man, who had knocked down a dinner with his gun, or caught a fish by angling from the rocks, invited a neighbour to dine with him, the invitation always ran 'bring your own bread'. Even at the Governor's table this custom was constantly observed. Every man when he sat down pulled his bread out of his pocket, and laid it by his plate.

The hardships described by Tench were in striking contrast with the open-air feast observed by Lieutenant Colonel Godfrey Mundy around the shores of Sydney harbour half a century later in 1846 (*Our Antipodes: Or Residence and Rambles in the Australasian Colonies*; 3rd edn, 1852):

> one pursuit peculiarly congenial to the tastes of the people—a pastime half jaunting, half sedentary; a little sea-air, a very little personal exertion, and a large amount of gastronomic recreation [is] oyster-eating. Every inch of rock from Sydney to the Heads is thickly colonised by these delicate shell-fish; that is, every inch would be so peopled, but for the active extermination incessantly going on. On any fine day parties of pleasure-and-oyster-seekers may be seen proceeding by water or land, furnished with the necessary muniments for an attack, or actively engaged in it. A hammer and a chisel, an oyster-knife, a bottle of vinegar, and the pepper-pot, with a vigorous appetite, sharpened by the almost impregnable character of the foe—such are the forces brought into the field, and the inducements to distinction. It is needless to add, that the garrison are quickly shelled out of their natural stronghold.

Early farming at Liverpool, NSW
Joseph Lycett (c.1775–1828)
Raby, A Farm Belonging to Alexander Riley Esqr,
New South Wales 1826
hand-coloured aquatint; 23.3 x 33 cm, plate mark
From the Pictorial Collection

(Mundy confessed that he had 'enrolled' himself more than once in an expedition of this kind, and only regretted that he 'had stomach' for only one-half of the luscious victims demolished by his companions.)

The newcomers observed with interest, wonder and sometimes abhorrence the food culture of the Aborigines—but their European minds were largely unconditioned to comprehend either the new land or its people. The ancient arts of hunting and gathering might have turned the famine into feast—and managed to conserve some of the oysters for later generations. But the newcomers would hunt and gather in their own way.

The agonising wait for the Second Fleet ended in June 1790, with both elation and disappointment: the ships brought much-needed supplies, but also more mouths to feed. Again, in such conditions, food was a question of survival, with little concern for refinement, even among the officers. Cooking facilities were primitive, though suiting the circumstances.

DIGGING IN

The desperate food shortages of the first few years were quickly overcome by a combination of shipping and farming. By 1792, fruit and vegetables were flourishing in the Parramatta region to the west of Sydney Cove. Maize grew well, and small quantities of wheat and barley were produced. Two years later, agriculture was commenced on the fertile Hawkesbury river.

(top)
Laying the ground to seed
S.T. Gill (1818–80)
Autumn c.1847
watercolour; 29.3 x 21.9 cm
From the Pictorial Collection

(bottom) A Chart of the Three Harbours of Botany Bay, Port Jackson and Broken Bay Showing the Ground Cultivated by the Colonists with the Courses of the Rivers, Hawkesbury, Nepean &c. ... by R. Scott
Scale [ca. 1 : 450 000]; 12.4 x 20.2 cm
(Newcastle on Tyne: Mackenzie & Dent, [1817?])
Rex Nan Kivell Collection; from the Map Collection

(opposite page, from top)
S.T. Gill (1818–80)
Summer c.1847
watercolour; 29.3 x 21.8 cm
From the Pictorial Collection

Norfolk Island, a critical food source in the colony's early, desperate days
Thomas Seller
[*Settlement of Norfolk Island*], 1835?
watercolour; 28.5 x 33.5 cm
From the Pictorial Collection

It took some time to develop suitable strains for local conditions, and production was at risk from drought and flood. Flour, in particular, was often in short supply, or selling at exorbitant prices—and for decades it was not uncommon to add ground maize, boiled rice or other fillers to bread. In 1796 the wheat crop seemed sufficient for a year; but as late as 1810 it was again so short that the colony had to make bread from maize flour. Nevertheless within a few decades visitors were remarking the abundance of local produce in the market. As historian Alan Frost has argued (*Botany Bay Mirages*, 1994) the disappointments of the first four years were heavily outweighed by the 'striking rapidity of the colony's progress in the next ten'.

As the local produce became more plentiful, eating patterns were able to change from the early dependence on predominantly shipped-in stores. Gradually, locally produced food came to dominate and imports provided what could not be grown or manufactured in the colonies. Increasingly, regular sea routes brought more luxury goods. The wealthier settlers kept the best tables they could, and the few luxuries which landed alongside the salt meat, rice and other staples were eagerly snapped up. As shown by the *Sydney Morning Herald* of 19 December 1849, ships arriving in the colony brought supplies of nuts, dried fruits, spices and fancy goods to grace the festive tables of those who could afford them.

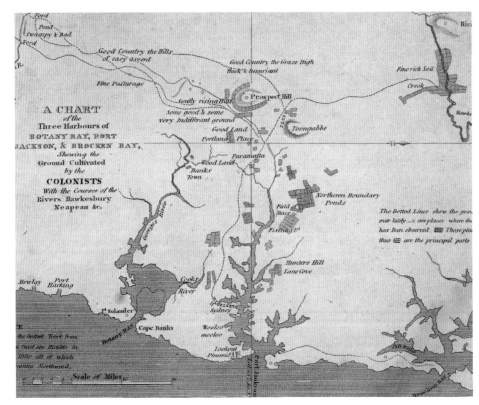

CHRISTMAS FRUITS—Mrs Creagh begs to inform her customers and the public generally, that in addition to her usual good supply of Groceries she has opened an excellent lot of Christmas Fruits, consisting of—
●Patras currants ●Muscatel raisins ●Sultana ditto ●Eleme ditto ●Jordan almonds ●Bottled fruits, &c.

LEARNING NEW SKILLS

For many decades, colonists had to be largely content with whatever could be grown locally or would survive the long sea voyage. Food was fuel—and to most people the joy of food was simply the joy of having *enough* of it. On the whole, there was little need for cookery books in the colonies in these early years, and those brought from home were of little use. The English books didn't teach survival cookery: how to make damper, or how to roast a haunch of kangaroo over a camp fire. Nor did they offer many ideas for enlivening monotonous ships' provisions, or making-do when wheat flour was scarce. Australian cooks had to learn new skills, and were doing so—as instanced by the kangaroo kebab and damper described in the published journals of Louisa Anne Meredith (1812–95) writing in the mid–nineteenth century.

AN AUSTRALIAN KEBAB

In *My Home in Tasmania During a Residence of Nine Years* (1852) Mrs Meredith made the following observations on the bush art of 'sticker-up cookery'.

MY HOME
IN
TASMANIA,
DURING A RESIDENCE OF NINE YEARS.
BY MRS. CHARLES MEREDITH.

IN TWO VOLUMES—VOL. II.

LONDON:
JOHN MURRAY, ALBEMARLE STREET.
1852.

The orthodox material here is of course kangaroo, a piece of which is divided nicely into cutlets, two or three inches broad and a third of an inch thick. The next requisite is a straight clean stick, about four feet long, sharpened at both ends. On the narrow part of this, for the space of a foot or more, the cutlets are spitted at intervals, and on the end is placed a piece of delicately rosy fat bacon. The strong end of the stick-spit is now stuck fast and erect in the ground, close by the fire, to leeward, care being taken that it does not burn. Then the bacon on the summit of the spit, speedily softening in the genial blaze, drops a lubricating shower of rich and savoury tears upon the leaner kangaroo cutlets below, which forthwith frizzle and steam and sputter with as much ado as if they were illustrious Christmas beef grilling in some London chop-house under the gratified nose of the expectant consumer. 'And, gentlemen,' as dear old Hardcastle would have said, if he had dined with us in the bush, 'to men that are hungry, stuck-up kangaroo and bacon are very good eating'.

Charles Edward Stanley (1819–49)
[*Charles Stanley's Puppy, Rattle, on Board
HMS* Windermere 1847]
watercolour; 25.3 x 17.6 cm
From the Pictorial Collection

THE 'ROAST BEEF MENTALITY'

A yearning for home cooking was a marked on board feature of the early long sea journeys out to Australia. Here, an 1840s voyage bears, along with its human passengers, beasts to stock the new land. Seventy-five years earlier, aboard the *Endeavour* (see opposite), Joseph Banks had used a food metaphor to evoke the sailors' homesickness, saying they suffered from a 'roast beef mentality'—yearning to be in safer and more familiar surrounds, eating that quintessentially English food.

FOOD AND HM BARK ENDEAVOUR

A fair idea of the kind of food that people on board the First Fleet had come to expect from day to monotonous day, and what they found on arrival at New Holland, can be gained from the records of Captain James Cook's voyages aboard *Endeavour*. The following text is taken from *Endeavour: Captain Cook's Journal 1768–71*. (CD-ROM, jointly published by the National Library of Australia and the Australian National Maritime Museum, 1998. Edited extract contributed by Stacey Smithers.)

SHIP'S PROVISIONS

In the late eighteenth century a ship's food staples consisted of salted beef and pork—salted because a strong brine solution killed most bacteria and therefore kept meat edible for several years. When it sailed from England, the *Endeavour*'s supplies also included: bread in biscuit form, bread in bags and butts, bread flour, beer, spirits (arrack), suet, mustard seed, raisins, dried peas, oatmeal, wheat, oil, sugar, vinegar, sauerkraut, malt, salt, saloop (a hot drink prepared from the dried tubers of certain orchids) and cheese. These foods would have pleased the tastebuds of most sailors who probably ate better on board than they did with their families at home.

To add variety to this diet, the beef ration was replaced with flour, suet and raisins once a week. From these ingredients the seaman could make a kind of pudding called a duff. As the cheese and butter rations spoiled rapidly, they were often substituted with oil and sugar. Additions to this basic diet were obtained wherever possible. In friendly ports, ships bought as much fresh produce as they could carry. In unknown parts, just about everything was experimental food to the crew.

(from top left)
While shipwrecked near what they named Endeavour River, Cook's crew foraged on such local delicacies as green turtle
Ignaz Sebastian L. Klauber (1753–1817)
Gezigt van Rivier Endeavour op de Kust van Nieuw-Holland 1795
engraving; 21.5 x 35.2 cm [plate mark]
From the Pictorial Collection

T. Prattent
The Bread Fruit Tree c.1800
engraving; 25 x 20.2 cm
Rex Nan Kivell Collection; from the Pictorial Collection

B. Raineri, after C.A. Lesueur
Animaux de la Nouvelle Hollande
(striped kangaroo and emu)
hand-coloured engraving; 24 x 32 cm
Rex Nan Kivell Collection; from the Pictorial Collection

(above) The *Endeavour's* galley was on the lower deck. The stove was made of iron, and the galley floor paved with brick to lessen the risk of fire. The stove was mounted on gimbals to simulate the ship's movements and stop the food from sticking by keeping food in motion. The stove could only hold the two copper boilers used to prepare stews, soup and boil meat. These boilers held between 25 and 50 litres each. The other side of the stove had spits for roasting and grilling—mainly for the officers and gentlemen. The stove had a small oven but bread was not baked on board. As fire was a constant threat, cooking would usually only take place in calm weather; in a violent storm the cook, John Thompson, probably doused the fire and the crew would have eaten cold food (Photograph courtesy of the *Endeavour* Foundation)

(below) One of Australia's first European gourmets
Joseph Collyer, after J. Russell
Sir Joseph Banks Bart. President of the Royal Society
stipple engraving oval; 10.4 x 8.1 cm
Rex Nan Kivell Collection; from the Pictorial Collection

The officers and supernumeraries aboard *Endeavour* would have supplemented their basic rations with supplies brought from home, including such items as spiced meat, other cheeses, dried fruit marmalade and their own store of wine. (Banks, for instance, had his own supply of good salt beef, salted cabbage, brandy, port and small ale.) Most of the livestock aboard ship also contributed to the table in the Great Cabin. The ship also had meatless days (Monday, Wednesday and Friday), on which one of the main meals consisted of boiled peas, oil, onions and pepper.

Baking bread on a ship increased the risk of fire so it was usually substituted with ship's biscuit ('hard tack'), made of wheat and pea flour in the Royal bakeries. It was baked two or more times to ensure that it would keep for up to a year. These biscuits were round, thick and stamped with a perforator (42 holes) in the centre so that the middle was more compressed and much tougher than the rest of the biscuit. This centre piece, called a 'reefer's nut', was usually eaten last or thrown overboard. To make eating biscuit more bearable, it was sometimes enclosed in a canvas bag and pounded with a marlinespike until it became a coarse flour, which was then mixed with chopped meat to make a stew, or with pork fat and sugar to make a cake.

Salted pork or beef (frequently called 'junk' or 'salt horse') was hard, fibrous, dark and glistening with salt crystals. More often than not, the meat was fatty and full of gristle and bone. It looked like a piece of mahogany wood. (Indeed sailors were known to carve boxes or model ships out of it, tossing these into the coppers in times of food shortage.) When cooked, most of the fat would float off, leaving the sailor with only a few salty fibres of edible meat. These fibres could be chopped up finely to make a 'sea pie' or made into a stew with raisins and biscuits. (Sailors were so accustomed to eating junk that they often resisted eating fresh meat taken aboard.)

A number of anti-scurvy agents were trialled on board *Endeavour*. These included sauerkraut (sour krout; literally 'sour cabbage')—a pickle of chopped cabbage packed in casks with layers of salt between layers of cabbage. Pickled cabbage was a variant. Portable soup was made by suppliers by boiling meat products until a thick residue was obtained. This was then reconstituted on

the ship by mixing it with water. It helped make wild vegetables more acceptable and gave the flavour of meat to the 'burgoo' on meatless days. Saloop was obtained from the roots of an orchid (*Orchis mascula*). New bulbs were washed with water, the fine skin removed, the bulbs heated in an oven, air dried and ground into a powder. This was added to boiling water and stirred to the consistency of jelly. Sugar or wine was added for taste. A rob of orange and lemons (made by boiling down orange juice to the consistency of syrup) was also served on board. Generally at sea, no priority was given to regularly obtaining fresh 'greens'—though Cook was an exception to this.

CATCH OF THE DAY

Wherever possible, Cook supplemented the ship's provisions with fresh supplies collected or caught along the way—including wild celery (added to pease or mixed with ground wheat and portable soup), scurvy grass, parrot pie, bananas, breadfruit, yams, kumaras (sweet potato), dog, rats and kangaroo. Throughout the voyage sailors ate an amazing array of fish, plants, birds and animals; when the crew caught more fish than they could eat the excess was salted and kept for later use. Turtles were caught on shore or harpooned at sea (female turtles often had the bonus of containing 100 or more sweet-tasting eggs). A dead cuttlefish found floating on the surface made one of the best soups the men had eaten. Stingrays were also eaten, served like steak, although everyone disliked their coarse texture. Birds were skinned, soaked in sea water overnight, boiled in fresh water and served with a savoury sauce. (These sauces made unfamiliar foods more palatable; one such popular sauce was made of coconut kernels fermented until they dissolved into a buttery paste and then beaten with salt water.)

For the period of the voyage botanist Joseph Banks and naturalist Daniel Solander were continually making scientific investigations of any animal that came to hand—from land, air or sea. Invertebrate or vertebrate, they examined, drew—and tasted—almost every one. Both Banks and Sydney Parkinson (the ship's natural history draughtsman) left comments in their journals about animals of particular note. (See extracts at right.)

FROM BANKS' JOURNAL

Kangaroo ... *Dind today upon the animal, who eat but ill, he was I suppose too old. His fault however was an uncommon one, the total want of flavour, for he was certainly the most insipid meat I eat.*

Sea squirts (cunjevoi) ... *howsoever disgustfull they may seem to an European palate, we found [them] to contain under a coat as tough as leather a substance, like the guts of a shell fish, in taste tho not equal to an oyster yet by no means to be despisd by a man who is hungrey.*

Giant clams ... *had 10 or 15 pounds of meat in them; it was indeed rather strong but I beleive a very wholesome food and well relishd by the people in general.*

Shark ... *Many shapes and sizes were caught when the ship was under sail, including a Great White: ... we made shift to have a part of him stewd for dinner, and very good meat he was, at least in the opinion of Dr Solander and myself, tho some of the Seamen did not seem to be fond of him, probably from some prejudice founded on the species sometimes feeding on human flesh.*

Turtles ... *are certainly far preferable to any I have eat in England, which must proceed from their being eat fresh from the sea before they have either wasted away their fat, or by unatural food which is given them in the tubs where they are kept ... Most of those we have caught have been green turtle from 2 to 300 pound weight ... two only were Loggerheads which were but indifferent meat*—sampling at Endeavour River, near present-day Cooktown, north Queensland

FROM PARKINSON'S JOURNAL

Stingrays [some] of an enormous size: one of them ... 239 pounds, and another 326. They tasted much like the European rays, and the viscera had an agreeable flavour, not unlike stewed turtle.

Parkinson also described the flesh of one ray, with a white belly and finely coloured polygons on its back, as tasting very like veal.

Many kinds of birds were also taken, and tested for their edibility, with only their heads, skin and/or legs left remaining:

... saw a great number of birds of a beautiful plumage; among which were two sorts of parroquets, and a beautiful loriquet: ... which we made into a pie, and they ate very well. We also met with a black bird, very much like our crow ... which also tasted agreeably.

EXPLORING

MUTTON, DAMPER & BILLY TEA

From the earliest days in the new colony, durability and portability had been established as the most important considerations in the provisioning of food. New arrivals venturing into the bush soon learned to their cost that their best chance of survival was to take their food (and often water) with them. Perishable food was of little use.

Even in the towns, limited local production and uncertainty of fresh supplies encouraged people to make do with a few durable and versatile provisions. Only basic recipes and kitchen skills were needed. The most useful style of cooking and eating was what most arrivals were already used to: sailors' and convict rations. The popular image of early Australian food as 'mutton, damper and billy tea' was fairly accurate—especially in the bush, where the normal weekly ration for a worker was 10 lb of flour, 10 lb of meat, 2 lb of sugar, 1/4 lb of tea, and salt. Potatoes and cabbage—the familiar food of home to many convicts and sailors—with perhaps a few other vegetables, provided some relief from durable stores, but only in the towns and on stations or farms.

The settlers had always shown interest in Australia's native food resources. Soon after landing, Captain Phillip had ordered a search for native vegetables, finding wild celery, spinaches, samphose, a small wild fig, and several berries which proved 'most wholesome'.

(above) Staple provisions of explorer and settler alike were meat, tea and damper
F.A. Sleap
Hume and Hovell Crossing the Murray in 1825 [188–]
wood engraving; 18.1 x 14.8 cm
From the Pictorial Collection

(right) Unlike the fox-hunting back home (Oscar Wilde's 'unspeakable in full pursuit of the uneatable'), the antipodean variation could furnish the basics of a tasty meal
Edward Roper (c.1830–1904)
A Kangaroo Hunt under Mount Zero, the Grampians, Victoria, Australia 1880
oil on canvas; 60.7 x 91.2 cm
Rex Nan Kivell Collection; from the Pictorial Collection

(opposite page, from top)
Frontispiece from Edward Abbott's *English and Australian Cookery Book* (London: Sampson Low, Son and Marston, 1864). The book's high literary tone is announced by the author's flowery dedication 'to His fair Countrywomen of the "Beautiful Land", the "blue-eyed daughters with the flaxen hair"...'

After George Stubbs
An Animal Found on the Coast of New Holland Called Kanguroo 1770
engraving; 23 x 26.5 cm
Rex Nan Kivell Collection; from the Pictorial Collection

Kangaroos, of course, were a ready source of red meat, fish abounded in the rivers and along the coast, and there were plenty of wild birds. With these the explorers and pioneer settlers soon began to supplement their rations. Likewise the imported gentry looked to native birds and animals to provide their sport.

EDWARD ABBOTT: 'AN AUSTRALIAN ARISTOLOGIST'

The earliest known Australian cookery book could be said to have been written by a culinary explorer: Edward Abbott (1801–69), of Bellerive, Tasmania. Abbott took over his father's extensive land holdings, prospered as a pastoralist and entered the Tasmanian Legislative Assembly in 1856. Later he moved to the Legislative Council. Like many of the early colonials, Abbott did his best to live like an Englishman. He was well read and an adventurous diner, prepared to try almost anything the country had to offer. Indeed, he styled himself 'an Australian aristologist' (one who is skilled in aristology—the art of fine dining). Abbott titled his work the *English and Australian Cookery Book: Cookery for the Many, as Well as for the 'Upper Ten Thousand'*. It was actually more of a culinary scrap-book of jottings, curiosities and recipes for colonial gentry than an organised handbook, and it is difficult to see it as having had much appeal to the free settlers and emancipists. Abbott drew most of his material from Britain, but also recorded some early Australian dishes—including the humble damper. He also gave lists of known fish in New South Wales, Victoria, South Australia, Tasmania and New Zealand, and described some of the native game animals.

Kangaroo was widely accepted both as survival food and as meat for the dinner table; Abbott gave about a dozen recipes for it. The simplest was of hindquarters larded with bacon, stuffed with a mixture of suet, breadcrumbs, shallots and herbs, slow roasted before a fire, basted with milk and served with 'good gravy, properly made' and currant jelly. Cold roast kangaroo made a fine hash for the next day; slices were gently reheated in a sauce of gravy, port, ketchup and lemon and served 'in a hot dish—silver, pewter or crockery, according to your circumstances'—with currant jelly sauce. Abbott's kangaroo pasty was a deep dish pie of marinated shoulder simmered with port, claret, shallots and herbs, baked under an inch of pastry. He declared it 'even more palatable' than a similar dish of venison.

Abbott also included two bush recipes given him by an 'old hand' in Tasmania. The first, pan jam, shows bush cooking at its best. Kangaroo tails were roasted in the ashes with the skin still on. When nearly done, they were scraped clean, divided at the joints, were put into a pan and fried gently with a few slices of fat bacon, some mushrooms and 'pepper, &c.'. Abbott considered this 'first rate tack'. And, if the etceteras were properly handled, he was probably right.

However the second of the old hand's recipes—for Slippery Bob—was a different matter, as suggested by the closing sentence of the recipe: ' "Bush fare", requiring a good appetite and excellent digestion'.

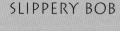

SLIPPERY BOB

Take kangaroo brains, and mix with flour and water, and make into batter; well season with pepper, salt, &c.; then pour a table-spoonful at a time into an iron pot containing emeu [sic] fat, and take them out when done.

—Edward Abbott, *The English and Australian Cookery Book*

NOTES.

During the early Colonial period Kangaroo meat was a regular article of food for pioneers. It is actually delicious, and much superior to ox tail soup when prepared in a similar way. However it has fallen from favor since tinned food etc has made the troublesome business of good cooking unnecessary to this lethargic nation.

THE SUNKEN STEAMER

Another dish, the kangaroo steamer, might have become a national dish. In Abbott's time it was said that 'of all the dishes ever brought to table, nothing equals that of the steamer ... No one can tell what a steamer is unless it has been tasted.' (Abbott, who was not very careful about acknowledging quotations, gave his source as 'Australia, by Melville'; though Lieutenant Mundy, writing from the 1840s, had also confirmed the popularity of the dish.) Edward Abbott was apparently fond of it himself, and gave three variations. One of them was a 'prize recipe', given with the explanation that:

> Mrs Sarah Crouch, the lady of the respected Under-Sheriff of Tasmania, obtained a Prize Medal for the above at the exhibition of 1862, and has allowed us to make public the recipe. The dish was partaken of by the members of the Acclimatisation Society, at the London dinner of that year, Lord Stanley in the chair. Several speakers commented on the goodness of the 'steamer'. Sir John Maxwell, a first-rate judge, pronounced it excellent, as a stew, and said that he should like to see it introduced into the Navy. It is understood that Prince Napoleon, one of the first gastronomers of the day, was desirous to acclimatise the kangaroo to France, for the sake of the 'cuisine' the animal affords.

Unfortunately, the dish's popularity was short-lived. Although the *Goulburn Cookery Book* gave a recipe for it in 1899 and Emily Futter gave another in her *Australian Home Cooker* (1922), after that it seems to have disappeared.

The steamer was simplicity itself as art-form: diced meat with no liquid, a minimum of flavourings, a tightly sealed iron pot left to cook very, very slowly at the side of the fire. The meat would steam or stew so gently that it could never stick. It would make its own gravy of pure meat juices. The fatless meat would be meltingly tender. More often, the dish was embellished with diced onion and bacon or salt pork and a little mushroom ketchup. It was served surrounded with sippets of toast and, for a 'steamer superlative', fried forcemeat balls 'as directed for roast kangaroo'.

Abbott listed other game with varying degrees of approval. He described emu as a very unctuous sort of food which much resembles coarse beef in flavour. Goat, he thought, was 'very good eating'. He did not like mutton birds (which were brought in from Bass Straight salted), but thought the eggs good. Black swan, when young, 'are tender, and if properly roasted, with good sauce, they are eatable; and that is all we can say'. He even listed wombat, noting that 'some persons like its flavour, others, again, decry it'.

BUSH TUCKER: MINA RAWSON

Native food resources were especially important for pioneer settlers and bushmen. Mina Rawson (1851–1933) gave one of the best accounts. Mrs Rawson had grown up in New South Wales, married in 1872 and moved to Queensland—first to a cattle station west of Mackay, then to a sugar plantation at Maryborough. When that venture failed she moved to Boonooroo, near Wide Bay, where the Rawsons pioneered a fishing station. This enterprise was hardly more successful, and the family depended heavily on the extra income Mina was able to earn by raising poultry, making hammocks and feather pillows, pickling shallots and writing. Moving to Rockhampton (where she became the first swimming teacher in Central Queensland) she continued to write books on cookery, household and farm management, 'fairy stories' and her own memoirs. For several years she was also social editor of the *Rockhampton People's Newspaper*.

Mina Rawson's cookery and household management books are still a delight to read. Though not well organised, they are full of sound, practical advice and written in a lively and engaging style with—despite the harsh realities of her early life—many touches of humour. Her 1895 reflections on the early bush kitchens give some idea of the hardships out of which the tradition of Australian country cooking grew:

> When I look at the old-fashioned camp-oven and the cross-handled chopper for mincing meat I often think the wives of those times served a martyrdom, and I believe they did just as much, if not more, cooking than we do, with our natty little American or gas stoves and our useful mincing-machines. One great art in cooking, especially in the bush, consists in making the best of poor materials, and in utilizing whatever we find ready to our hands, and in being able to use any oven or fireplace, even an open fire on the ground, with the ashes in which to cook the damper. Nowadays one is seldom called upon to cook by such primitive means, unless when camping out, or newly married, and in a strange land.
>
> —*The Antipodean Cookery Book and Kitchen Companion*, 1895; facsimile 1992

Mina Rawson encouraged women in the bush to learn from the Aboriginal people, and to try the kinds of food they ate. Few, she said, would refuse bandicoot, wallaby or kangaroo; she also recommended iguana (goanna) cooked in the Aboriginal fashion on the ashes—even carpet snakes roasted. No one who enjoyed oysters, she thought, should be put off by witchetty grubs, and there was 'a large brown grasshopper' which could be 'very good when parched'. Among vegetables, she recommended young pigweed as a substitute for lettuce or as a hot vegetable, and young shoots of the 'rough-leaved native fig' as a substitute for spinach.

While pioneers such as Mrs Rawson found that they could improve their chances of survival by learning Aboriginal techniques of hunting and gathering, others were less adventurous. A few had come to make an English colony in the antipodes; many had come to better their position or to escape conditions in Britain; some had come because they were given no choice. Whatever their ambitions now, their food traditions had been made in Britain and had come with them to the new country along with the clothes they wore.

By 1900, widespread interest in native food had all but died out, except for a few animals and birds regarded as game. Though there has been some resurgence of interest in the late twentieth century. (See 'Kullanteenee Bush Tucker' feature, p. 85.)

PARROT PIE

Hilda Cross, b.1902, lived on the land at Yarrowitch, near Walcha, NSW.

... we used to catch parrots ... Shoot parrots and make parrot pies. They used to smell lovely cooking on the open fire ... it would take [laughs] about a dozen parrots to make a parrot pie. Sitting down and plucking them was the big job. They were so tiny and the feathers so fine.

[We only ate] rosellas. There were others but the others were smaller than rosellas so they weren't worth getting hardly. [Parrot pie] was just cooked like soup, and put onion and thyme and parsley and things like that in it ... the bones used to be left on, and mother used to put a pie crust over it and you picked the bones yourself [laughs]. The same as you'd make a chicken pie, only it was dark flesh, but it was really nice. Not many people would like them now I don't think, but you were glad to get something that was fresh.

... [and] there were lots of hares ... they used to eat hares, and they were nice. I've often tried to cook one since but I never could cook it as nice as mother did ... She used to fry it ... it's very dark flesh and make a stew of it with onion and thyme and things like that, and we used the rabbits too ...

[Kangaroo] was nice ... lots of people ate kangaroo ... We [only] did during the Depression. We had kangaroo tail soup ... it was quite nice, except that it's sticky. You know, stick your lips together. It was thick. You didn't have to thicken kangaroo tail soup. It was thick itself. But it tasted very nice.

[In the summertime we ate] eels ... there was a lot of those ... Fry them in batter. You'd just boil them or steam them, but mainly fried in batter. They were very nice. I still like them. I think they have a better flavour than any of the other fish. It's just the thought of them with most people ... They can't stand the look of them, but they taste just as nice [as fish].

(above) One person's pretty polly is another's parrot pie
After John Gould & H.C. Richter
Rosella Parakeet (Platycercus eximius) (detail)
lithograph; vol. 5, plate 27, *Birds of Australia*
From the Pictorial Collection

LEARNING TO COOK

COLONIAL COOKERY, & THE RISE OF 'DOMESTIC SCIENCE'

'MEAT, DAMPER AND TEA' HOLDS OUT

Lucy Drake's *Everylady's Cook-Book* —'A Guide to All Young Brides. A Friend to All Housekeepers' (2nd edn) (Melbourne: Fitchett Brothers, 1926). Miss Drake was another of the teachers who had studied at London's National Training School for Cookery. She became head of the Domestic Arts department at the Swinburne Technical College, Victoria, in 1914. Her books were revised and kept in print by her former assistant, Dorothy Giles, becoming kitchen companions to thousands of Australians

One hundred years after the early colonists had faced starvation the country had achieved a remarkable turnaround, and Australia was being described as a land of plenty. The international cookery section of *Mrs Beeton's Cookery Book and Household Guide* (1892) commented:

> The only difference in provisions in Australia may be said to be that the supply is so far more abundant there than here. Almost everything we consume can be found there cheaper and more plentiful, and many of the luxuries of English food are within the reach of the poorest of the colonists.

Meat was generally good in quality, and very cheap. Fish was plentiful and, as we have seen, oysters were not considered a luxury. Fruit and vegetables were easy to grow and were therefore to be had in abundance.

The book gave a selection of Australian recipes: oyster soup, kangaroo tail soup, parrot pie, roast wallaby, broiled cod steaks, pumpkin pie, preserved watermelon rind (though not of the variety now popular) and a moulded pudding of creamed rice with poached apricots. It declared that:

> neither roast wallaby, which might be compared to [English] hares, nor parrot pie, not unlike one made of pigeons, would be found at the dinner-table in the hotels, but up country they are esteemed as very nice dishes.

An Australian journalist, Richard Twopeny, writing in 1883 (*Town Life in Australia*; facsimile edn 1973) painted a similar picture of Australian cuisine as an abundance of local produce which was 'somewhat coarse, albeit wholesome enough'. For the working classes food was 'immeasurably better and cheaper' in Australia than in England, though he thought the upper classes were better provided for in the old country.

The abundance of meat, fruit and vegetables, however, had not meant that colonial Australians had become great cooks. The survival diet of meat, flour and tea—once dictated by military convenience, shortages of supply and the need for portability—had become the food of choice or habit.

Twopeny was in fact scathing of the standard of Australian cookery, even in the wealthy households, and dismissed the common excuse that good cooks were scarce:

> It is not merely because it is difficult to entice a good cook to come out here. If he really wants a thing, the wealthy colonist will not spare money to get it; but how can you expect a man who—for the greater part of his life—has been eating mutton and damper, and drinking parboiled tea three times a day, to understand the art of good living?

Thus the wealthy were content with 'occasional grand dinners' and plain family meals. For their cooks this probably meant long periods of culinary boredom producing plain food for unappreciative employers, punctuated by short bursts of panic as they struggled to produce half-forgotten high-class dishes for uncultivated—but critical—diners.

The middle class had less culinary choice: large families were obliged to stretch their more moderate incomes, and having a cook did not always mean having good dinners. As Twopeny commented:

> The usual female cook at 12s. a week is not even capable of sending up a plain meal properly. Her meat is tough, and her potatoes are watery. Her pudding-range extends from rice to sago, and from sago to rice, and in many middle-class households pudding is reserved for Sundays and visitors. A favourite summer dish is stewed fruit, and, as it is not easy to make it badly, there is a great deal to commend in it. At the worst, it is infinitely preferable to fruit tart with an indigestible crust.

In a sense, it was actually the poor who did best. By all accounts, they did not eat well—but better than they would have done in Europe. Food was still 'fuel'—but rough fuel was cheap and plentiful.

GOOD FOOD, POORLY COOKED: THE AUSTRALIAN LEGEND

Twopeny was not the only writer to praise the quality of colonial food while deploring its standard of cookery. The causes of this paradox were undoubtedly more complex than he suggested, and are still being explored by historians. The development of food production and distribution arrangements, food and kitchen technologies, communication media and marketing—and, of course, the sources from which Australia drew its population—were all important factors, as were the changing role and status of women.

(*above*) 'Grand dinner style' poultry and game (left to right, top to bottom): barded and roast partridges, roast Surrey fowls, larded guinea fowl, roast plovers, stuffed capon à la mayonnaise, roast gosling and roast pigeons. According to this work's 1923 preface, Mrs Beeton's books 'have appeared among the wedding presents of brides as surely as the proverbial salt cellars, and thousands of grateful letters from all English-speaking countries testify that they have often proved the most useful gifts of all'.
Mrs Beeton's All-About Cookery (new edn)
(London/Melbourne: Ward, Lock & Co, 1923)

(*left*) S.T. Gill (1818–80)
Butcher's Shamble, nr Adelaide Gully, Forrest Creek [1852]
lithograph; sheet 15.7 x 19.3 cm
Rex Nan Kivell Collection; from the Pictorial Collection

MEAT, THE STAPLE DIET

Of course meat is the staple of Australian life ... A working-man whose whole family did not eat meat three times a day would indeed be a phenomenon. High and low, rich and poor, all eat meat to an incredible extent, even in the hottest weather. [And not in] mere slices, but in good substantial hunks. —Richard Twopeny

KEROSENE-TIN CAMP FIRE COOKERY

The 'bush school of cuisine' persevered well into the twentieth century, and for rural workers and others continues in sundry ways still ...

To make a stew and have it hot for dinner, though you are away at work ... get a 7lb. treacle tin, then take a rabbit, and, after dressing it, cut it up, and soak it overnight in salt and water to remove the blood. In the morning put it, with a little corned beef, potatoes, onions, and seasoning (if you have it), into the treacle tin. Knock a nail hole in the lid (to let out the steam), and put it well down into its place. Put the lot into a kerosene tin, with water nearly up to the top of the treacle tin, and set on the fire to boil while you have your breakfast. Leave your tin and fire safe after breakfast and go to work. When you come back you will have a hot dinner, all ready cooked. If water is scarce, and you cannot spare enough for the kerosene tin, fill the treacle tin with water, bring it to the boil, and then bed it well in the ashes and leave it. If you suffer from indigestion, take a seidlitz powder going to bed. You will be alright in the morning, and will remain so till you overwork or overload the stomach again.—Bush Cook.

—Mary Gilmore, *The Worker Cook Book*, 1915

(above right) This painting, showing kangaroo awaiting preparation for the bush table was used as frontispiece to Russel Ward's influential 1958 text *The Australian Legend*
Augustus Earle (1793–1838)
A Bivouac of Travellers in Australia in a Cabbage-Tree Forest, Day Break [c.1838]
oil on canvas; 118 x 82 cm
Rex Nan Kivell Collection; from the Pictorial Collection

One of the causes was already staring Twopeny in the face. In the second half of the nineteenth century Australians were busying themselves with shaking off their convict origins. Morality and law-and-order continued to be important themes, but public debate was increasingly concerned with economic and, later, even cultural development. Political leaders were looking towards nationalism. Lifetime habits, however, are not so easily dispensed with. As historian Russel Ward pointed out in *The Australian Legend* (1958), by 1851 rather more than half the white population were convicts, emancipists or 'currency' lads and lasses. Many of the remainder were working-class people who brought with them no tradition of good cookery. The next few decades saw the emergence of what Ward called the 'Australian legend'—a national image of the itinerant male bush-worker as a kind of ideal Australian, even for the great urban populations. And this worker's rations were meat, flour, tea, sugar and salt.

It was no wonder that the upper-class colonists gave little leadership in the improvement of Australian cookery: many of them were emancipists made respectable by newly acquired wealth, but with little appreciation of food beyond a certain reverence for abundance and display. Perhaps they were the customers Peate and Harcourt of George Street, Sydney, had in mind when offering up the following for sale in the *Sydney Morning Herald* of 14 October 1885 (most of the following would have been tinned):

> Breakfast Delicacies, Game, Ham and Chicken, Pork, Savory [sic] Veal and Ham Pâté, Oxford Brawn, Salmon Cutlets, Truffled Pâté de Foie Gras, Truffled Birds, Larks, Quail, Woodcock, Snipe, Plover and Partridge, Preserved Game, Fish, Meats, Fruits, Tongues, Sausages, Soups, &c., of every description.

By the late nineteenth century there was growing interest in cultural development in the colonies—public health, education and the arts were increasingly coming under public discussion. Even the high-minded *Sydney Morning Herald* (7 January 1891), which had hitherto shown little or no interest in home life, was ready to tackle the problem of Australia-at-the-table:

> The curse of Australian life is bad cookery. The person who first coined the aphorism on this subject—'The gods send food, but the devil sends cooks'—only crystallised the experience of multitudes in the matter ...

Indeed, there seems to have been general agreement about what had to be done: girls and women had to be taught to cook—and provided with useful recipes.

(above) Preserving fruit
From Mrs Anna L. Colcord's *A Friend in the Kitchen, or What to Cook and How to Cook It* (Melbourne: Signs Publishing, 1912)

(below) Typical settler's abode, equipped with meagre utensils
S.T. Gill (1818–80)
Interior of Settler's Hut 1845
wash; 11.2 x 19.7 cm
From the Pictorial Collection

A BUSH LARDER

A bushman's hospitality is proverbial; in fact, if it be rejected, or even if when passing an acquaintance fail to drop in to the hut, and fail either to be helped or to help himself to the food he finds hanging up in the bags from the roof (a larder intended to circumvent the ants, though not always successful), he will not improbably give his would-be host much offence ... If you find the stockman away from home the orthodox custom is to go in, hand out the meat and bread, put the 'billy' (a tin quart saucepan) on the fire ... throw in a quant. suff. of tea and then take your fill, always remembering to rake the ashes back again over the blazing logs, and to place the viands back in their proper places. —Percy Clarke, The 'New Chum' in Australia... *(London, 1886)*

COOKERY TEACHING AND 'DOMESTIC SCIENCE'

The first cookery teachers, not surprisingly, came from Britain. Most had been trained in the National Training School for Cookery in London, and were proud of their qualifications. The teachers included Ramsay Whiteside, Annie Fawcett Story, Harriet Wicken and Margaret Pearson—all of whom gave lessons in Sydney or Melbourne in the 1880s. Behind them came a wave of other teachers who they themselves had trained in Australia—such figures as Amy Schauer, who taught for more than 40 years at the Central Technical College in Brisbane, and Amie Monro, who taught in Sydney.

The first attempt to teach cookery in schools was short-lived, however. Ramsay Whiteside began classes at rooms in Macquarie Street, Sydney, in May 1882, but the venture proved too expensive for the education authorities and the school was closed at the end of 1885. A few years later, Annie Fawcett Story established classes at the Fort Street Public School and was successful in integrating what became 'domestic economy' into the New South Wales curriculum before she moved on to Victoria to become Directress of Cookery there.

In its broadest sense, 'domestic economy' meant management of the household. Mrs Beeton used it in this sense in her chapter 'Arrangement and Economy of the Kitchen', where she discussed kitchen layout, equipment, the foods in season, and how they should be preserved and stored. The term also had a more pointed meaning: the thrifty management of household resources. As Harriet Wicken put it in her own textbook, *The Kingswood Cookery Book* (1888):

> It is the duty and pleasure of every woman at the head of a household to consider how to get the greatest amount of comfort for her family with an outlay proportionate to her means. There is a great deal of difference between economy and parsimony.

(Though, looking back at some of her recipes, one might wonder how well she understood this difference—for some of them were economical to a fault.)

Domestic economy became 'domestic science' about 1912. The name change was in part an attempt to elevate the status of the subject within the curriculum, but also reflected the faith of the age in progress through science. Frederick Taylor in America promulgated his 'scientific management' in 1911. Gas cookery was well established; electricity had just been introduced to Sydney and promised a new age of domestic convenience. In other States the pattern was similar. (Western Australia, for instance, introduced 'domestic economy' to the State school curriculum in 1900, then changed to 'domestic management' in 1905—and girls who took it were exempted from elementary science.)

The elementary course in cookery taught by Annie Fawcett Story was made up of 12 lessons printed on large cards and hung up for all to see:

> Lighting fires, cleaning stoves and flues, washing cookery utensils, scouring tables, buying and keeping stores; Baking and roasting meat and the pudding which generally goes with it; Cooking vegetables; Boiling and stewing meat; Frying and broiling; Soup making; Cooking fish; Pastry making; Puddings; Bread and cakes; Invalid cookery [for those in illness, convalescence or poor health generally]; Breakfast and tea dishes.

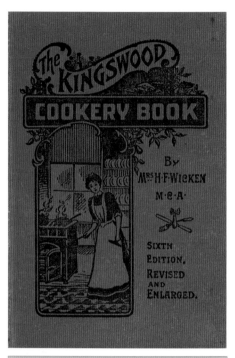

FISH À LA TASMANIA

Cook 1 codfish in the oven, and flake it up; mince 3 ozs fat bacon and shred of onion, and mix it in with 1 oz bread crumbs and pepper; mix into a paste with 1 teaspoonful of anchovy sauce and 1 egg; roll into balls, cover with egg and bread crumbs, and fry in very hot fat; pile in a dish, and send melted butter sauce and anchovy to table with them.

—Harriet Wicken, *The Kingswood Cookery Book*

Harriet Wicken's *The Kingswood Cookery Book* (6th edn) (Melbourne: Whitcombe & Tombs, 19—)
In its preface the author declared: 'I do not seek a place for [this book] amongst high-class or elaborate works, but I desire to make it a guide for everyday needs, to teach housewives to vary their menus, so as to give an additional charm to home life'

FROM A DOMESTIC SCIENCE EXAM PAPER

The following questions, from two different three-hour examination papers, indicate the eclectic mix of themes studied. (They were recorded in the *New South Wales Legislative Assembly Votes and Proceedings*, vol. 2, 1869.)

An attentive domestic science class in Newtown,
New South Wales
Brady Collection; from the Pictorial Collection

1. How may a good wife render her home attractive to her husband?
2. What are the most common modes of adulteration practised in daily food?
    State the evils which arise from the practice referred to.
3. What are the advantages of cold water bathing?
4. What differences are effected upon animal food in baking, as distinguished from roasting?

❖

1. Under what circumstances may presence of mind be valuable in a house?
2. What are the advantages and uses of Salt in the preparation of food?
3. What causes induce Husbands to frequent Taverns?
4. In choosing colours for clothing, what shades are desirable, and what objectionable? Explain why.

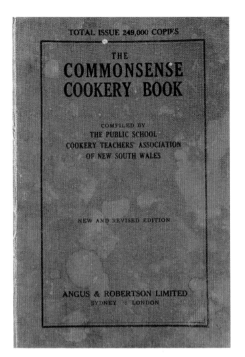

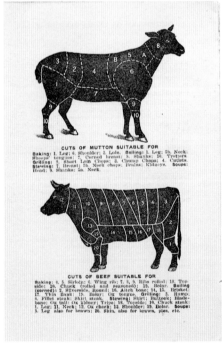

The no-nonsense appearance of the best-selling *Commonsense Cookery Book*, and a page explaining meat cuts (Sydney/London: Angus & Robertson, 1941)

Hannah Rankin, who became supervisor of cookery after Mrs Story left, set down the theoretical part of the course in a little booklet called *Principles of Practical Cookery for School Pupils*. Soon afterwards, the teachers of the West Redfern Cookery School collected the recipes into another small work (*West Redfern Cookery Book*, 1908) which no doubt proved useful to many young women. It is an interesting and historically important book. Its 95 recipes—all of the 'plain cookery' sort—provide one of the clearest records of what dishes a competent Australian family cook was expected to be able to make around the turn of the century—from tea-and-toast, to steak-and-kidney pudding. (Most other contemporary cookery books included many novelties and recipes for special occasions—making it hard to tell which dishes were actually in common use.) The Redfern book set out a dictionary of cookery terms in one page: *boquet garni* [sic], *caramel*, *soup croutons*, *garnishing croutons*, *Patna rice*, *blanch*, *tepid*, *clarified fat* and *panada* were apparently the only special terms a plain cook needed to know.

A charming feature—and one quite unusual for an early cookery book—was the inclusion of several photographs: the first staff of cookery teachers trained in New South Wales, and the cookery students at the Fort Street, West Redfern, Forrest Lodge and Wollongong schools. More charming still was the first page of the book, given over to the cookery school mottos:

> 'Instead of being regarded as a servile employment, Cookery should be considered an Art and a Science.'

> 'Have a place for everything, and keep everything in its proper place.'

> 'Well clean the corners, and the middle will clean itself.'

> 'The three chief characteristics of a good housekeeper are CLEANLINESS, PUNCTUALITY, ECONOMY.'

> 'Anything worth doing is worth doing well.'

> 'WASTE NOT, WANT NOT.'

THE COMMONSENSE COOKERY BOOK AND OTHERS

In 1914 the New South Wales teachers compiled a new recipe book for their students: the now-famous *Commonsense Cookery Book*, with a much larger selection of recipes—though all still of the plain sort. The recipes overlooked no detail, however small, and were set out in numbered steps so simple that no diligent cook could fail to make the dishes properly. And again the 'golden rules' explained what was required of a diligent cook: accuracy, cleanliness, punctuality, orderliness and economy.

The *Commonsense* was revised and expanded many times over the next six or seven decades to keep pace with changing ideas about food. It remained, however, a conservative and quaintly old-fashioned book; its purpose was to teach good, plain family cookery rather than to follow food fads. Countless thousands of brides took it to marriage as their first cookery book (along with any collections of old favourite recipes copied out of their mothers' scrapbooks) and continued to use it for many years, even as the recipes aged. By the time a special edition was issued—'on the occasion of the visit to Australia by Queen Elizabeth in 1954'—more than half a million copies of this classic had been sold.

Newer textbooks came along, and other States developed their own equivalents of the *Commonsense* book—such as Victoria's *Approach to Cookery* (1962) for elementary students, and *Cookery the Australian Way* (1966) for advanced cooks. Generally, their approach to the subject was the same: first, the need for rigid adherence to a body of rules about cleanliness, accuracy, orderliness and economy; second, the importance of nutrition; and third, systematic teaching of the basic methods of Anglo-French cookery, with a selection of typical dishes.

If, however, as the West Redfern book explained in 1908, cookery was an 'art' as well as a 'science', it is difficult to find in any of these books much actual *passion* for food—or much teaching about how to enjoy it. Australians had been taught to cook scientifically, and food was still—first and foremost—*fuel*. Not until the 1980s were students much encouraged to think of food as a rich expression of cultural diversity.

COLONIAL RECIPES

A 'good plain dinner' in colonial times—say, of roast beef, potatoes and boiled greens, followed by a suet, rice or sago pudding—was a dinner prepared along British lines. A higher-class dinner, with a full range of dishes and all the proper accompaniments, demanded British or Anglo-French recipes. From early days, British cookery books were available for those who wanted—and could afford—them. It was not uncommon for immigrants to bring one in their chest of household possessions. In the *Sydney Morning Herald* (of 4 July and 3 November 1855) the bookseller and stationer W.R. Piddington advertised such works under the heading 'Cookery books, the best'. These were: *Mrs Rundell's Domestic Cookery* (new edition); *Soyer's Modern Housewife*; *The Illustrated London Cookery Book*; and *Kitchiner's Cook's Oracle*.

Yet among those who took an interest in the science and art of cookery there was a belief that such British books were 'unsuitable' for Australian conditions. The different climate, the limited availability of manufactured goods and the hazards of storing perishable foodstuffs certainly pointed to a need for a different diet and different cookery techniques—though not all colonials thought about it in those terms. Few differences in technique show up in early Australian recipes—beyond the 'survival' foods of campfire cookery and the occasional strengthening of a jelly with extra gelatine to help it withstand the summer heat. The belief that British recipes were unsuitable was probably more influenced by attitudes towards Britain—as seen, for example, in the cocky independence of the Australian-born 'cornstalks' and their superiority over 'new chums'.

By the end of the nineteenth century a good market had developed for cookery books which could claim to have been written for Australian conditions. As we shall see, what showed up as the main differences between them and the British books were the fruits of exploration and adaptation.

Little Flinders Street, Melbourne, bustling with the activity of provisioning. Somewhere among the items coming in by sea would have been cookery books from Britain
[*Scenes in Melbourne*, 1880]
hand-coloured wood engraving; 31.6 x 23.2 cm
From the Pictorial Collection

SUNDAY DINNER

... Sunday we ... all had to eat in the dining room, the white starched table and ... I can remember this quite clearly, there was one bottle of DA beer for mum and dad, and this old Aunt Jule ... and one bottle of lemonade for my brother and I ... That was the only bottle of lemonade I can remember we ever had in the house, was Sunday dinner, and Sunday dinner was very important. The big roast sirloin and dad would carve it at the end of the table and all the vegetables would be brought in, the vegetable dish covered up, and mum served the vegetables round, and if you wanted anymore, you could help yourself, but everybody had to sit up and eat their meal correctly. That was one day that they insisted you did the right thing, because that was the only day, I suppose, that the whole family ate together.

... you had to eat every vegetable that was put in front of you. You didn't have any likes or dislikes. If you didn't like it, there was no other vegetables made ... there was always baked potatoes and baked pumpkin, and I can remember cauliflower, but they didn't dress it up with cheese and all the things we do today. It was always served with white sauce and [there was always a] green vegetable—if not two, but always one—and the greens were in one dish and the baked vegetables in the other ...

... and of course [there was] always sweets. There was a sweet every night of our life ... and Sunday dinner you had ... [an] extra choice sweet, I might say. You might have baked rice custard or that sort of thing during the week, but on Sunday you had something extra: fruit salad was always cut up and had for Sunday—with cream ... —G.T., b.1905

SABBATH DINNERS.

(from top) A family meal in Victoria
in the early 1940s
Photograph by Australian Information Service
Drouin Town and Rural Life during World War Two;
from the Pictorial Collection

Artwork from Mrs Anna L. Colcord's *A Friend in the Kitchen, or What to Cook and How to Cook It*
(Melbourne: Signs Publishing, 1912)

THE SUNDAY ROAST:
A STUDY IN DOMESTIC ECONOMY

The Sunday roast was a good case-study in 'domestic economy'. The ritual went something like this.

1. *Sunday.* Take a large piece of meat (a 'joint'). Trim off the scrappy bits and put them into the stock pot. Remove any excess fat and boil it down for dripping (if done carefully, the dripping would be good enough for pastry or even cakes). Roast the meat and serve it up with pride (and, of course, baked vegetables and gravy).

2. *Monday.* Cover the used part of the joint with mashed potatoes, brown it in the oven and serve it up again (with a gracious smile).

3. *Tuesday.* Slice some of the remaining rare meat thinly, moisten it with gravy, add a dash of Worcestershire sauce, a squeeze of lemon and maybe a bit of onion, and reheat it gently. It is now *hash*—or, if there is company, you may call it *réchauffé*.

4. *Wednesday and following ...* There might be enough left on the bone to carve off some neat pieces to season, batter and fry. The joint has now become *meat fritters*—or, if the occasion needs improving, epigrams

Now, if the meat is still 'sweet', it is time to mince the remains. The mince can be seasoned, moistened with gravy (if there is any left from Sunday), topped with mashed potato and baked as *shepherd's pie*. Or you can season and press it into shapes, coat them with crumbs and fry them as *savoury cutlets*. If the amount of mince is smaller than your family's appetite, you can add some left-over boiled rice to make *rice cutlets*. (The bone, of course, can go into the next stock pot.)

On the other hand, if the weather has been warm and you cannot honestly still call the meat 'sweet', then you are in for a *curry* (with onions, apples and curry powder).

This is perhaps a severe case of 'economy', yet it does not exhaust the possibilities. A good cook had dozens of different ways of 'using up' the remains of a joint of beef or mutton. And, with the arguable exception of the curry, they could be very good.

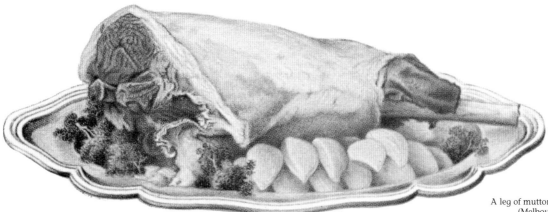

A leg of mutton from *The Australasian Cookery Book*
(Melbourne: Ward, Lock & Co, 1913)

DR MUSKETT'S CULINARY PRESCRIPTION

Marion Halligan

We read a lot about food in newspapers and magazines these days. I don't mean recipes, telling us what we might go out and buy and cook for dinner, I mean food as news. As good news and bad news. We all know what I mean: butter bad news, margarine good. The demon fat. Polyunsaturated oils better, mono-unsaturated not so good. Hang on ... it's not so simple ... there are bad fats and good fats ... and is hydrogenation all that desirable? ... and who paid for the research that decided polyunsaturated oils were the answer to all our problems ... surely not a polyunsaturated oil company? ... And what about Popeye getting superhuman strength from scoffing cans of iron-rich spinach when in fact there was only a tenth as much iron in it as advised (some researcher had put the decimal point in the wrong place). And all that shellfish we didn't eat because of the danger of cholesterol ... wasn't there something dodgy about that research too ... ?

And so we read our daily papers, trying to keep abreast of the news of which food will save us, which will kill, especially as the protagonists tend to swap places. The promises of the good life turn out to be contingent, or hollow, contradictory, or just plain false. Salvation through food is proving harder than that through faith or works. Both are matters of occasions of sin. Weren't we all better off when we ate what we could get and were grateful for it? In moderation of course, and after a hard day's work that kept us fit—and alas, there's the problem, we live in such plenty that it may destroy us.

But paying attention to what we eat is not a new phenomenon. And maybe it's salutary to look at some older advice. Philip Muskett's for instance. He was a doctor in Sydney a hundred years ago, and had strong ideas on the health of the colony which he proselytised in books. He thought we should follow a New York scheme of loading the slum children of Sydney on to barges in the hot weather and towing them out beyond the Heads into the fresh air, thus reducing infant mortality, a scheme which makes you think Sydney pollution is of no recent date. But mainly he was concerned with food and cooking, in two books, *The Art of Living in Australia (Together with Three Hundred Australian Cookery Recipes and Accessory Kitchen Information by Mrs Harriet Wicken*, 1892; reissued in facsimile edition in 1987) and *The Book of Diet* (1898), the latter an expansion into university lectures of some of the main concerns of the former.

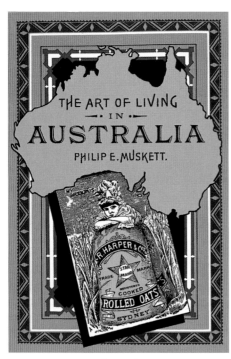

(from top)
Marion Halligan (detail of a photograph from the Canberra 'Seven Writers' series, 1990)
Photograph by Brenda Runnegar
gelatin silver photograph; 25 x 20 cm
From the Pictorial Collection

Facsimile edition of Muskett's pioneering work; accompanying recipes were provided by Harriet Wicken
(Kenthurst, NSW: Kangaroo Press, 1987)

You could sum these up in three ideas: salads, wine, and the morality of cooking. His emphasis on salads comes from a comparison of the climate of Australia with the same latitudes in Europe; Australia he says 'is practically Southern Europe' and so our diet should resemble that part of the world's. Australians, he worries, in a similar climate to the Italians, eat ten times as much meat as they do. We should eat a lot more vegetables and much more fish. In other words, we should look to the Mediterranean diet for our models—this in books published in the early 1890s. (His idea of climatic matching is expanded by Michael Symons in *The Shared Table*: *Ideas for Australian Cuisine*, 1993. Symons adds parallels with Asia: Chinese food in Sydney, Thai in the Far North, and French only in Melbourne.)

Muskett insists that the best way to eat vegetables is in salads, not the terrible English kind, of lettuce shredded with a sharp knife, sitting in its own water on a flat plate, that we still were eating in my youth, but a French salad, the leaves whole, washed or wiped and dried, dressed with good oil (he recommends Crosse and Blackwell's olive) and a much smaller quantity of good wine vinegar. This is not difficult, the problem is the salad herbs, the chervil, tarragon, parsley, chives, the mustard and cress or watercress, which are impossible to obtain. We should be eating rocket, and lamb's lettuce (or mache). Celery and radishes as a garnish are a poor substitute for this variety, but better than nothing.

Our national dish, he said, should not be tea and damper, but a macedoine of vegetables, a vegetable curry, or 'a well-concocted salad'. Both of Muskett's books spend a lot of pages on the detail of good salads, and recommend that we demand the raw materials of our suppliers. I remember talking to Stephanie Alexander, about ten years ago I suppose, when she showed me her own restaurant garden with its variety of lettuces, which she had to grow because none were available commercially; now of course there is a good range even in supermarkets. But it's a gruesome thought that it took a century for Muskett's ideas to come into practice.

Dr Muskett's suggested strategy for keeping hubby out of the bars has perhaps not proved entirely successful
Geoffrey K. Townshend (1888–1973)
[*Boys in the Bar*], 192–
wash; 38.5 x 53.9 cm
From the Pictorial Collection

We acted a bit sooner on his second great recommendation, which is that wine should be our national drink, and 'take the place of all other liquids, since it is essentially wholesome, hygienic, restorative, and cheering'. It should be a light wine (not a sherry or port, that is) so that people can drink a lot of it and quench their thirst, without '"fatiguing" either head or stomach'. Much better for us than tea. Though a little coffee can be restorative.

Donald Friend (1914–89)
From 'Ayam-Ayam Kesayangan'
(Donald Friend Diaries)
From the Manuscript Collection

As well as being good for us as a drink, wine will do wonders for the economy. He points out that Paris, with its population of two-and-a-half million, would drink in 12 days the whole wine production of Australia. Since Australia had a population of three million, imagine how good it would be for the wine industry if it had to produce a Parisian quantity over 12 months; 'what a magnificent future only awaits its calling into being'. He describes the sunny smiling landscape of prosperous vineyards turning Australia into a kind of paradise.

Wine is also involved in the moral dimension of cookery, along with the education of young women. If they are taught to cook well, to provide a delicious and varied diet, it will keep their husbands at home, they won't need to go off to the pub and drink spirits. 'Millions of our English-speaking race are living this life without the slightest glimmering of what domestic content might be theirs. Surely the word "home" for the artisan should signify something more than a place where he is badly fed'. Drinking wine with this excellent well-cooked food will add to the happiness and harmony of the home, and is the best preventative of drunkenness, much more likely to work than preaching total abstinence. Moreover, Muskett suggests that much too can be learned from Gallic habits of thriftiness: 'materials which the English housewife throws away as useless, her French sister skilfully converts into toothsome and nutritious food'.

Muskett of course is a fellow of his times, when men were breadwinners and women were housewives. Nevertheless, his advice, if you remove the gender specifics, is excellent. And a great many of us are acting on it these days. People do stay at home eating delicious meals and drinking wine with them, though none of that comes from learning cooking at school. What is bizarre is that it should have taken us so long to catch on; it needed two wars in Europe and vast migrations of peoples before we learned what a simple reading of Muskett 100 years ago would have taught us. What melancholy pig-headed ignorance to have lived in so long.

KITCHEN TECHNOLOGY:
FROM CAMP OVEN TO INDUCTION COOK-TOP

Australia's second complete cookery book was not about making food and cookery more suitable for Australian conditions, but about using new technology in the kitchen. Alfred Wilkinson's *The Australian Cook* (1876) was written to promote the use of gas cookers which had recently been introduced in Melbourne and Sydney. (Wilkinson was then chef of Melbourne's Athenæum Club.) The new cookers quickly became popular and were among the first of a long line of innovations in the Australian kitchen.

Massive developments have occurred across the whole range of kitchen technology, with an accompanying and profound impact on both the foods we eat and the way we prepare them. A brief sketch of the developments might be indicated in such progressions as the evolution from the Coolgardie safe to the freezer; the colonial oven to the microwave; the gas stove to the induction cook-top; the gas grill to the barbecue; the advent of the pressure cooker, the electric frypan, the electric rice cooker and electric wok; mixing appliances (from basic basin and whisk, to multi-function food processor); the evolution from early ice-cream churn to modern ice-cream maker; and from simple convenience food such as tinned meat to so-called 'gourmet' convenience preparations. And of course in the changing structure of the kitchen itself.

Oil and gas cooking stoves (shown *above* and *left* respectively) challenged the more traditional wood-burners, and were themselves later challenged by electrical cookers, though gas has held out as a favourite
Australasian Ironmonger (1 April 1890, and 1 November 1888)
From the Pictorial Collection

(from above left)
A housewife evidently delighted
with her modern electric refrigerator, as depicted
in the pages of *The Australian Women's Weekly*
from August 1956

Mrs C.R. Rudd at 'Merrigang' sheep station,
Charleville, Queensland, in 1956. Her coke-fired
kitchen range is supplemented by a cake-mixer run
from a 32-volt home electricity generating unit
Photograph by W. Brindle; Australian News and
Information Bureau
From the Pictorial Collection

According to the original Departmental caption, the
photograph at *right* represented 'the typical all
electrical kitchen in a modern Australian home'
Australian News and Information Bureau
From the Pictorial Collection

According to the 1950s promotion,
the modern Australian home would
incorporate provision for the
'preparation cycle' of the kitchen
routine, and would feature an electric
mixer, stove, and quick-boiling
electric jug, with stainless steel sink,
easy-wipe benchtops, and perhaps a
radio for accompaniment. Some of
these modern appliances were slower
spreading to country kitchens.

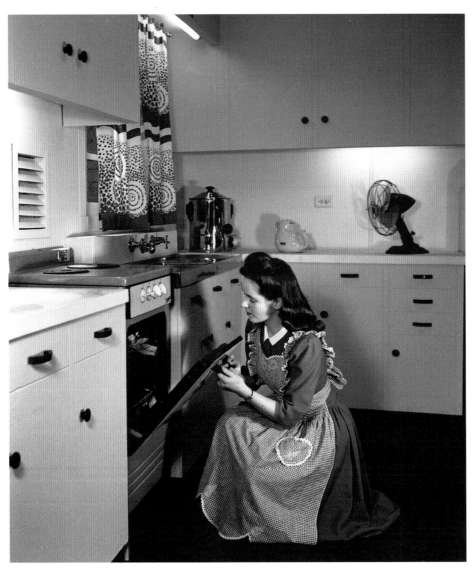

TOWN & COUNTRY
CITY & BUSH COOKS

From the early days of white settlement Australia seemed destined to become a society of urban dwellers. In 1820, just over half the non-Aboriginal population was living in towns. The proportion fell dramatically during the years of rural settlement and gold fever, then the cities regained their dominance—and have not lost it since. By 1981, 86 per cent of Australians were living in cities or towns. Yet, as Russel Ward showed, the outback (or 'up-country', as many colonials called it) was a powerful influence on the Australian way of life and on what many people came to think of as the 'Australian character'.

By the early twentieth century, the legend of the Australian bushman had become popular in both town and country, and was to dominate the way Australians thought about themselves for decades. (A second, though less popular stereotype was of the urban larrikin.) According to Ward, the typical Australian man was seen as a practical and independent-minded person, rough and ready in manners, and intolerant of pretentiousness or officiousness. He was a great improviser, ever willing to 'have a go' at anything, yet easily contented with 'near enough'. He was hospitable and always stuck to his mates. This entirely male legend of an idealised (and sometimes idolised) Australian figure was able to emerge because of the much greater proportion of males among those who first went up-country and, perhaps, because of male dominance of public life.

'City and bush': the bushmen with damper and billy tea, the town ladies with fancy food and fine bone china
'Five O'clock Tea: In Town and in the Bush'
From the *Australasian Sketcher*, 22 January 1876
From the Pictorial Collection

This figure had two important consequences for the history of food and cookery. First, it kept alive—and even romanticised—the idea of meat, damper and billy tea as the common food of Australia. In the country they were the foods of necessity; in the cities meat, flour, sugar and tea were also the staple provisions, especially among the working classes. Fresh fruit and vegetables, colonial butter and cheese were the extras, while imported hams, tinned and dried fish, dried fruits, pickles, and sauces were the luxuries. Long after bread had replaced damper, and tea was made in tea-pots, the serving of dainties, kickshaws and 'fancy food' was generally something of an embarrassment to 'real' Australians. A second consequence of the Australian legend was that it tended to push into the background the prior claims of Aboriginal people, and the pioneering contribution of women—both in the cities and in the bush. More recent scholarship has begun to redress this imbalance, to rediscover the food of the bush and to focus on the various roles of women—recognising that the Australian nation was shaped as much in the home and the neighbourhoods as it was in the outback and the parliaments. Whether to please or to civilise their menfolk, it was overwhelmingly the women who shaped Australian cooking.

SELF-SUFFICIENCY

... You had your home and you grew everything you possibly could for a living. All your vegetables, and you made your own butter and killed your own meat—and lots of times went without meat, just vegetables and butter was all you had because you couldn't afford to kill many stock. And you could only kill in the wintertime because you had to salt it all: you had fresh meat for a couple of weeks after you killed and then the rest was salt meat till that was finished. So in the wintertime the neighbours used to kill between each other. One would have half or quarter or something like that and then pay it back when they killed. That was how they managed ... —H.C., b.1902

Woman inside Settler's Hut
Australian Consolidated Press; Charles Kerry
Tyrrell Collection; from the Pictorial Collection

(below) Kickshaws and 'fancy food'—anathema to the
Australian legend
Reproduced from *Mrs Beeton's All-About Cookery*
(Melbourne: Ward, Lock & Co, 1923)

To say that Australians generally rebelled against dainties and fancy food is not, however, to say that in culinary matters they were unadventurous. The harsh and brutal discipline of the convict era left a legacy that some would say persists to the end of the twentieth century—a sullen submission to authority from which there was seemingly no escape, accompanied by an underlying resentment of it. Thus ordinary Australians resisted petty bureaucracy, made a folk hero of Ned Kelly and promoted a sanitised version of larrikinism as a national trait. Their attitude to food was not much different: they accepted the boredom of rations without enthusiasm, and rejected much instruction in the finer points of cookery. We earlier noted the wide variety of cookery traditions that had migrated to Australia. The middle and upper classes' ideal had been that body of cookery best described as 'respectable'—inspired by the studied carelessness of the securely wealthy, yet 'solid' rather than 'lavish'. In the Victorian era, cuisine was to become as riddled with useless rules and expectations as the etiquette that weighed down those trying to better (or hold) their place on the social ladder. When Isabella Beeton codified all this in her monumental work (*The Book of Household Management*, 1861), she took a page to explain the two modes of properly making toast (dry, and 'hot buttered'). Confronted with the multiplicity of rules necessary for a respectable table, what else would a true colonial do but brush these aside as 'unsuitable'? And, if taken by the mood, throw any leftover vegetables, along with the obligatory meat, into the batter for a traditional toad-in-the-hole?

COUNTRY COOKS

If independence, persistence, adaptability and willingness to take a chance were ideal 'Australian' qualities, then country cooks—whether male or female—thoroughly earned a place in the Australian legend.

Distance from towns, poor roads (or often no roads at all) and slow, cumbersome transport meant that supplies were limited and infrequent. Meat was salted or cured as the only practicable way of preserving it without refrigeration. When fruit was abundant it was preserved or made into jam; some vegetables could be preserved or stored. Eggs were preserved in lime water or waterglass, by rubbing with vaseline and storing in bran, or by various other methods. Milk—if any was available—quickly went sour, though its life could be extended by scalding. Even city housewives had to do this, as one wrote in the *Sydney Morning Herald* of 12 February 1908:

> Everyone knows that boiled milk will keep sweet twice as long as unboiled, but few people know that you can keep milk sweet indefinitely by boiling it up every 12 hours. Of course the milk is poorer after every boiling, but still it is milk, and good for puddings, and indeed many poor mothers bless this thin milk when they want an early cup of tea and the milk doesn't come till 6.30 or 7.

Meals had to be prepared from what was available, and little could be left to waste. This often imposed severe limits on what could be done and sometimes meant that food became boring. But it also encouraged a marvellous spirit of inventiveness and adaptability: mutton was dressed up as goose; rabbit served up as turkey; beef as duck. And sometimes the 'ham' was mutton or kangaroo. Jam was made with passionfruit skins and 'ginger' was made from melons, marrow, pears or even chokos. Cakes and puddings were made with eggs if there were plenty, and without if there were not. Concoctions of milk jelly or cornflour custard were turned into 'whipped cream'. If there was no

(above) Mrs Robert Wharton making a cake in a country kitchen during the 1940s, and (left) a perhaps somewhat contrived interaction in a country store. An ironmonger's corner in the same establishment would have provided many of the basic kitchen utensils
Both photographed by the Australian Information Service
Drouin Town and Rural Life during World War Two; from the Pictorial Collection

THE TRIP IN TO THE STORE

... it took a week to go to Walcha [the nearest town] and back with the horse team ... [my father] did that once a year and we used to buy three 150 [pound] bags of flour, and I can't remember how many bags of sugar, and that used to do us for ... almost the 12 months mostly. —H.C., b.1902

Old stalwart: the wood-burning stove
Donald Friend (1914–89)
From 'Ayam-Ayam Kesayangan'
(Donald Friend Diaries)
From the Manuscript Collection

THE KITCHEN STOVE

[Our kitchen] was only tiny, like a tiny little skillion. It wasn't very big. There was no stove in it ... they only had the open fire and mother cooked in a camp oven. I can just remember ... helping gather the baking bark to put on top of the oven and then she got a Younger stove ... I think it might have been 1912 ... and it sat in the big fireplace. It wasn't done in: it was just sitting in a big fireplace and she cooked in that, but the kitchen only had a table then for washing up and shelves to put the crockery on and that sort of thing, and we carried our water from the creek ... —H.C., b.1902

red berry jam to enrich the queen pudding for Sunday, it would be enlivened with stewed rhubarb. Almost any home-made jam could be turned into a sauce for steamed, boiled or baked puddings—especially useful when milk could not be spared for a custard sauce. Marzipan was made with breadcrumbs, coconut and essence. Yeast for bread came from almost anything that would ferment (though a combination of hops and potatoes was a favourite).

KITCHENS

Early kitchens were primitive, and improvements came only slowly: there were still country homes (not too far from towns) without the benefit of electricity as late as the 1950s. Cooking was hard work (try whipping whole eggs for a sponge cake with a fork or even a wire whisk!). Wood-burning stoves were messy, labour intensive and tricky to regulate. (You could judge the temperature of an oven by placing in it a piece of white paper or some flour sprinkled on a plate; the colour change would show how hot the oven was. Experienced cooks had another way: they would poke their bare arm through the oven door for a few seconds.)

LINING THE KITCHEN WALLS

... we used to get sheets of clean newspaper and make up a paste out of flour in a big pot and rub the paste onto the paper with a bit of rag or cloth or something and stick it on the wall. This used to go on every 12 months ... Just before Christmas. —V.D., b.1928

OPEN FIRE COOKING

... [And] we used to cook on the open fire ... Mother used to bake the bread, mixed up the dough, you know, and put yeast with it and then it would rise in a bowl and then she'd roll it out on a board with flour until it was a soft sort of dough, then she'd put it in the camp oven, hang it on the fire, put the lid on it and put coals and charcoal and stuff on top of the lid, leave it on for about an hour; turned out beautifully. —V.D., b.1928

(left) Country women preparing a meal at a picnic race meeting, 'Talbingo' station, Southern Highlands, NSW. The various State Country Women's Associations have a longstanding tradition of producing practical cookery books with often enviable print runs
Photograph by J. Fitzpatrick
From the Pictorial Collection

(below) Camp ovens, as seen in the 'kitchen' at Junction Rally, Wentworth, NSW, 1992 (detail)
Photograph by Narelle Perroux
From the Pictorial Collection

COUNTRY COOKERY BOOKS

We have already seen what Mina Rawson had to say about the trials of country cooking. In the late nineteenth century she wrote several practical cookery and household management books for country housewives. Another work—the *Goulburn Cookery Book*, compiled about 1899 by Jean Rutledge of Bungendore for the Anglican Diocese of Goulburn—was a favourite in New South Wales for decades. Ella Winning of Moree, New South Wales, published another country cookbook (*The Household Manual*) in 1899. The *Australasian Pictorial Home and Farm Manual* of 1885, an impressive-looking reference book for life on the land, also included a recipe and household hint section. (Though its claim to being Australasian was slight: it was actually a thoroughly American book with a short local article on 'pleuro-pneumonia in cattle' at the back.)

Another source of cookery books has been the various Country Women's Associations (CWAs) of Australia—established in New South Wales in 1922 and still serving country women and children nationwide. These associations were keenly aware of the need for recipes that were thoroughly practical for country kitchens, yet able to add interest and variety to family meals and social occasions. Through most of the twentieth century the CWAs have produced a steady stream of cookery books. Among the well known ones are the *Coronation Cookery Book* of New South Wales (first issued in 1937 to celebrate King George VI's coronation) and Western Australia's *C.W.A. Cookery Book and Household Hints*, which has seen more than 40 editions since about 1936. The Bundaberg CWA Branch first produced its cookery book in 1928. The 'treasured recipes of the country women of the Esk Valley' in Tasmania have also been kept in print for decades in another charming little book.

Cooking at Yarralumla shearing shed in
the ACT, in 1957
L.J. Dwyer Collection; from the Pictorial Collection

A SHEARERS' COOK

*I used to cook for shearers ... and that wasn't
very easy ... At 22 I was getting two pounds
to cook for six men, myself and the family...
three meals a day, and a cup of tea before
breakfast, and morning and afternoon teas.*

*[Morning and afternoon teas would be] Scones
and biscuits and cake. One old lady said I
made the cakes too light. She said, 'make
them a bit heavier'. I said, 'how would I do
that?' 'Oh,' she said, 'put more flour in. That's
good enough for shearers'. So it's not much
wonder shearers kicked over the traces. They've
gone too far now, but they didn't have it all so
good [then] ... It was meat and vegetables for
every meal ... They just had meat and
vegetables for breakfast, and a pudding and
some kind of a meat dish for lunch, and the
same for tea ... They'd have bread and jam
and things like that for tea, but not always
pudding. But my word it kept you going. You
didn't have time to sit down at all, and all the
washing up there was to do... —H.C., b.1902*

One popular way of helping—and encouraging—country women to put
plenty of variety in their families' meals was the recipe calendar. Designed to
be hung up on the kitchen wall like (or instead of) an ordinary calendar, it
gave a different recipe for each day of the year. The South Australian *Calendar
of Meat and Fish Recipes* (1956) and the New South Wales *Calendar of Puddings*
(1931) are good examples.

Today most country kitchens are equipped with deep-freezers, electric stoves
and microwave ovens. Many have food processors or electric woks. And
country supermarket shelves look little different from those of a city
supermarket of similar size; country cooks have ready access to much the
same range of fresh and processed foods. Yet that certain mystique and
romance of country cooking which has always attracted city-dwellers, lingers.
It is the same the whole world over. Perhaps too much supermarket
convenience, too much variety and too much sophistication occasionally sets
off an inner reaction—triggers some deeply buried, inherited memory that
once all people lived the simple life on the land. The desire for good plain
food, simply prepared, becomes irresistible. Only freshly picked young corn,
quickly boiled and eaten off the cob with a little butter, salt and pepper will
do. Or corned beef with cabbage, tender carrots and a well-made parsley
sauce. And then, perhaps, a gramma pie, fresh from the oven—for the very
few who still remember it. And who would not trade a dozen loaves of hot-
bake for a single slice of old-time country bread, toasted on a wire fork before
the coals of a farmhouse fire.

TOWN COOKS

Whatever romance has been conjured up by the legends of the bush, the reality for most Australians has been life in the cities. As Michael Cannon put it (*Australia in the Victorian Age*, 1975, vol. 3, introduction), white Australians had:

> established themselves at a few convenient seaports around the endless coastline, hurled themselves against the intimidating interior, and retired baffled, broken and defeated to their starting points. Leaving only the bravest, toughest or most stupid behind them to break open the land, every man of reasonable common sense took the softer option and became an entrepreneur or labourer in the coastal cities. Here, even at its roughest, life could be made cosy.

Or so, perhaps, they thought. The very successful were able to plant large gardens between their grand houses and the badly laid-out, unlit, undrained, muddy streets stinking with horse manure, kitchen garbage and sewage. The merely wealthy gained some protection by moving to the best land surrounding the cities and establishing 'desirable suburbs'. The working classes had little choice but to endure the crowded, unsanitary conditions of the inner city, and the result can be read in the appalling disease and death rates of the late nineteenth century.

Kitchens and cooking arrangements were as varied in size and amenity as the houses themselves—though as a rule, as little money was spent on the back of houses as possible. Consequently kitchens were small in proportion to the houses they served: badly designed, and poorly equipped. As journalist Richard Twopeny quipped (*Town Life in Australia*, 1883):

> As far as kitchen fittings are concerned, Biddy has to content herself with a table, dresser, safe, pasteboard and rolling-pin, and a couple of chairs.

(Doubtless there was also a colonial oven and a few cooking utensils.)

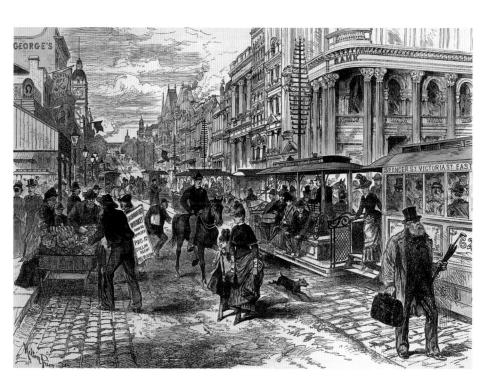

Late nineteenth-century Melbourne, with touters of bananas and whisky
Melton Prior (1845–1910)
Collins Street, Melbourne
From *Illustrated London News*, 11 May 1889
hand-coloured wood engraving; 25 x 33.5 cm
From the Pictorial Collection

GADGETS; AND THE SERVANT PROBLEM

At the beginning of the twentieth century kerosene was a common fuel for lighting—and wood for cooking and water-heating. From about the 1890s an increasing range of gadgets and appliances began appearing on the market—bigger and better stoves, smaller and cheaper stoves, ice chests, mincing and grinding machines, steamers and many others. Gas stoves came on sale in both Melbourne and Sydney in 1873, soon followed by other gas kitchen appliances including water-boilers, grillers, broilers and toasters.

The appearance in 1907 of a little book called *Thermo-Electric Cooking Made Easy* (oddly enough published in the remote mining town of Kalgoorlie, Western Australia) was a clear sign that a kitchen revolution was under way. By the mid–twentieth century, electricity had become the normal power for lighting, and gas and electricity were rapidly replacing wood for cooking. Nearly all urban houses had hot and cold running water, though in some houses it was still necessary to carry water from one room to another.

Another major change affecting middle-class families was the necessity of managing without domestic servants. Although a general shortage had driven up the wages commanded by cooks and other domestics, their shortcomings and misdemeanours had become a perennial theme of complaint by their employers. As the *Sydney Morning Herald* lamented in its 'Page for Women', 14 April 1909:

> After marriage the higher life is impossible. Servants are the asphyxiators of the soul. They become staple talk. I have watched a girl deteriorate from a maiden to a wife, from a wife to a bondswoman. First she talked Shelley, then Charley, then Mary Ann.

Despite her failings, the 1901 census found that nearly 22 000 private households still employed at least one 'Mary Ann' each. During the next two decades, however, the proportion of women employed in private service declined rapidly: by the 1930s the employed household cook belonged to another age as far as most families were concerned. Whether the growing shortage of domestic help hastened the advent of labour-saving devices—or whether the modernisation of kitchens enabled households to dispense with hired help—is still not entirely clear. Girls and women were increasingly attracted to jobs in the burgeoning factories, though wages and conditions there were far from ideal. At the same time, the new gadgets and conveniences were massively advertised and often promised freedom from the annoyances of servants. Whatever the causes, women (for the lot nearly always fell to them) began to take an increasingly keen interest in their kitchens and in the amount of labour they required. And the new gadgets were as attractive to those who had never had the luxury of servants as to those now struggling to do for themselves.

(from top)
A domestic services recruitment pamphlet from about 1930. The number of women and men wishing to take up such employment had declined generally from the end of World War One, an incentive (along with the increased expense of maintaining such staff) for more household gadgets and easy-cooking preparations
From the Pictorial Collection

Electric kitchen gadgets from the 1920s: griller, waffle iron, toaster, milk or water heater, coffee percolator, tea pot with infuser, and hot plate. The impulse for kitchen appliances has continued unabated, with an abundance of plastic in more recent decades
Reproduced from *Mrs Beeton's All-About Cookery* (Melbourne: Ward, Lock & Co, 1923)

Washing up in a dish, kettle gently boiling on the hob: domestic life in the restrictive dimensions of an Australian kitchenette in the early 1920s
Sydney Mail, 30 December 1921
From the Pictorial Collection

THE MARKET

Another factor seeing rapid change was the efficient distribution of food, moving away from the very early days of supply from government stores. Governor Bligh had established Sydney's first formal market in 1806 in an attempt to enforce orderly and fair trading in farm produce. A few years later it had moved away from what was then 'the middle of High Street' (now George Street) down to the south end (where Market Street now crosses). As the city continued to expand a new hay and corn market was established in the area still known as Haymarket. By the late nineteenth century, however, the central markets were beginning to look decidedly tatty beside the new town hall and cathedral, and there were many other pressures for reform. A new fruit market was built on the site that had been home to Paddy's Market for half a century or more, but the site was wrong for its new purpose. In what proved to be a grand folly, a magnificent new structure was erected where the old central markets had been: the Queen Victoria Building was opened in 1898 and was an immediate economic failure. The soul of the city markets had fled.

Harold Cazneaux (1878–1953)
Old Belmore Markets c.1905
(Paddy's Market, Haymarket, NSW)
photograph; 40.4 x 50.6 cm
Cazneaux Collection; from the Pictorial Collection

THE CELLAR COOLER

[We used the area] underneath the house—that would have been made today ... into a terrific cellar for wines and things because it was cool—now we kept the meat down there and milk, or anything that you want for breakfast was kept down in the cellar, because it was cool—it was underneath the house and no sun got to it, so that was the coolest part in the house ... —G.T., b.1905

(above) A bird's-eye view of Sydney in 1888, with some green areas seen to be still adhering to the west. The ships depicted brought an ever-increasing range of foodstuffs to Australian tables and exported an increasing array of local produce
By M.S. Hill; published by Samuel Crump Label Co. (detail)
chromolithograph; 51 x 75.5 cm
Rex Nan Kivell Collection; from the Pictorial Collection

(opposite page)
Selling rabbits in Moruya, NSW, in the early 1900s. Vendors also hawked these, along with fish, bread, milk and vegies in the suburbs of the major cities
From the Pictorial Collection

Livingstone Hopkins (1846–1927)
[*Chinese hawker Carrying Shoulder Baskets, the Rocks, Sydney*] 1886
sepia etching; 30 x 19.9 cm [plate mark]
From the Pictorial Collection

An 1880s ice-cream cart
From *The Australian Sketcher*, 25 February 1882
From the Pictorial Collection

Early on, bulk stores had also sprung up around the wharves to dispose of the cargoes of incoming ships. Traders were often prepared to sell in 'quantities to suit private families'. Retail stores followed, and neighbourhood grocers popped up to sell an array of 'provisions' including tea (ranging in quality from 'ration' to best Hyson, Congou and Souchong), coffee, sugar (from 'ration' to white 'snowdrop'), spices, dried fruits (currants, raisins, muscatels, prunes, figs and dates), almonds and Barcelona nuts, pickles, bottled sauces, bottled fruits, fresh and salt butter, colonial and imported cheeses, hams, bacon, salt meat, salt and tinned ('fresh') fish, rice, sago, patent groats and other meals, flours—and a wide range of other practical household items (not least among them being candles).

An 1873 Sydney directory listed a total of 357 grocers, 233 butchers, 130 milk distributors, 107 bakers and 134 fruiterers and greengrocers—though the directory may not have reached far enough out into the suburbs to give a complete picture. As wealthier residents moved to the suburbs, new arrangements were needed—Chinese market gardeners began selling their produce from carts; butchers, bakers and dairies delivered to households in horse-drawn carts. Itinerant hawkers and barrowmen sold fish, rabbits, wildfowl and other game. (See feature opposite.)

The production and distribution of meat, fish and dairy produce remained major public health problems until well into the twentieth century. Abattoirs and dairies were often filthy and disease-ridden; the sale of diseased meat and tuberculous or adulterated milk provoked frequent public complaint until adequate public health laws were enacted and enforced. Shoppers learned to be wary.

The central markets of all Australian states in time gave way to arrangements more suited to modern, sprawling cities and the practicalities of suburban living. But virtually all cities and major towns have retained some form of retail market for selling fruit, vegetables (and sometimes fish) to those who enjoy the bustling environment, the variety, and perhaps the prices.

Just as the challenges of country living inspired a steady stream of practical country cookery books, the opportunities of city living provoked a flood of its own. Cookery books from the country and the cities had much in common, for there was no clear line of demarcation between country and city food. But they also had their differences: country books spoke quietly of resourcefulness and making-do; city books such as *Ideal Australian Home Cookery* (from the mid-1930s) showed suburban housewives how to serve up dainty meals. But the themes were often bolder, and sometimes brash. A small selection of city titles over the years suggests the story:

XXth Century Cooking and Home Decoration (1900)
Something Different for Dinner (1936)
Australian Cookery of Today (1940s)
The Chef Suggests (1949)
Better Cooking ... by Gas (1959)
Cooking Better Electrically (1960s)
Barbecue Cooking (1970)
The World Guide to Cooking with Fruit and Vegetables (1973)
Ted Moloney's Easy Gourmet (1978)
Particular Picnics (1985)

HAWKERS:
ICEMAN, BAKER, GROCER, RABBITO, FISHO ...

DOOR TO DOOR

Gladys Timbs, born in the eastern Sydney suburb of Woollarah in 1905 when the area was still partly bushland, recalls the deliveries of the early 1920s.

... In the summertime ... you'd get a block of ice one day, and the next day if it was very hot the ice would be gone ... the iceman [only came] twice a week ... if you wanted anything [more] you would have to drive to the ice works ...

... The baker came with his horse, and he'd walk up Holdworth Street and the horse would walk ahead of him and stop at each customer, and the baker would come in with his bread and the basket ... I think it was twopence halfpenny a loaf ...

... And I tell you who else used to come around ... it was a great treat to go out with a plate when the rabbito come round, and he'd have the rabbits hanging with their two legs joined together, and they were one and threepence a pair, and he'd cut the heads off and throw it to the cats that would be following him along ... and there was nothing, no wrapping it up—he'd skin it and he'd put it on the plate ... you ... brought them in, with a tea towel covered over it ...

... The baker had all the bread in the basket, and he just came and handed it to you and you took it off him and gave him the money. There was ... nothing wrapped

... and then, of a Friday, there would be a horse-and-cart would come around and you'd buy fish, [they would] be calling out 'fisho', and you'd go out with the plate, a clean tea towel over it, and ... buy what fish you wanted off him, and he'd cut the heads off and clean it and give it to you and away he'd go.

... So, we got deliveries then that we don't get today ...

The Corner Shop.

KITCHEN COMPANIONS

DOING THE BOOKS

The history of Australia since white settlement is dominated by documents—and therefore by the kinds of activities which generate documents. It is no accident that more is known about the public side of Australian life—about the acts and policies of government, the formation of public companies, births, deaths and marriages, property purchases and events which have attracted the notice of newspapers—than about the private lives of ordinary people. Although many private papers have survived and found their way into public collections, very often it has been because the people concerned were not ordinary, but public figures in some capacity.

The history and culture of a people are shaped as much by what they do in private as by what they do in public, yet until recent years the documentary evidence of private life has generally been patchy and circumstantial. In the area of food and eating there are good records of what foods were offered for sale, but not of what manufactured food products were actually bought, or by whom. There are also substantial records of published recipes—and fairly good records of the kinds of recipes that were put out by food manufacturers and grocery stores to promote sales—but very little reliable evidence of what recipes people actually *used*. Libraries, museums and other cultural institutions house a wide range of material, including oral records, on which researchers have increasingly come to draw in their efforts to construct a clearer picture of the home life and culture of earlier generations.

Some knowledge of what officers and convicts ate during the initial 'survival' years of the colony has been pieced together from scattered proclamations, official correspondence and private diaries. Australian cookery books do not really start until late in the nineteenth century: probably few households had them before that. Some of the officers' wives would have brought with them one of the popular English books—or perhaps purchased one here from a W.R. Piddington, but the books' influence over daily affairs in the kitchen would have been slight. The day's cookery had to begin with the ingredients that were on hand or available for purchase: the range was often very limited, and the English books were not much good when it came to ringing the changes on salt meat.

Literacy, too, was a factor. It was not simply a case that cooks and working-class housewives could not read. In fact, basic literacy rates in the colonies were surprisingly high (Alsop, 1993; Oxley, 1996). It was rather that cooking was part of an oral culture: what knowledge the cooks and housewives had of kitchen craft had been handed to them by word-of-mouth and by example. They did not rely on written records: cookery was learnt in the kitchen. When faced with an unfamiliar task, a cook's instinct would not be to pore through a cookery book for directions—but to ask advice, avoid the task, or rely on her wits—with whatever results.

BUSH POT

An A.W.U. man's 'special' dinner cookery. —Put a tablespoon of water and a little fat in a saucepan and lay in 2lb. of good steak. Cut and wash a cabbage. Put in a layer of cabbage and some pieces of thin bacon, then more cabbage and more bacon till you have all you need, bacon being the last thing put in. Cover with a close lid and set to steam. While this steams, wash well some rice, and boil in salted water till cooked. Drain and return to the fire to steam as dry as possible. Serve the steak and cabbage in the centre of a dish surrounded by the rice, and pour over the gravy after removing any overplus of fat.

—Mary Gilmore (ed.), *The Worker Cook Book*

(above) The Worker Cook Book, edited by Mary Gilmore
(Sydney: The Worker Trustees, 1915)

(opposite page)
The friendly neighbourhood store, still holding out today though besieged by supermarkets and cut-throat marketing
Donald Friend (1914–89)
The Corner Shop
From 'Ayam-Ayam Kesayangan'
(Donald Friend Diaries)
From the Manuscript Collection

The willingness of town and country cooks, male and female, to have a go at any unfamiliar kitchen task, without regard to the rules of England, was a powerful shaping force on the cookery and eating habits of ordinary Australians. It can be summed up in three principles.

> 1. Meat dishes should be simple and tasty. This did not demand herbs, spices and aromatic vegetables; they were complex. It generally meant plenty of salt, pepper 'if liked', and bottled sauces and pickles.

> 2. Vegetables had to be eaten for health—they did not always have to be enjoyed.

> 3. Only a few basic recipes for puddings, cakes and sweets were really needed—but they could be varied almost endlessly according to what was on hand.

SHARING EXPERIENCE

The willingness of cooks to share their experience was another shaping force. Many girls learnt to cook under their mothers' instruction. Neighbours helped each other. The art and lore of bush cookery were passed on in bits when occasion demanded—perhaps it was a new chum's turn to make the damper, or the only water for miles was muddy and the new chum could watch an old hand clarify it with camp fire ashes.

Much of the information that was passed by word-of-mouth in the early days has now been lost. Some was circulated by letter or written into household notebooks—most of that, too, has been lost. Even when printing had become relatively cheap and newspapers common, few working-class people regarded print as a way of sharing their culture with others. An exception to this was the Labor newspaper, the *Australian Worker*, the women's pages of which were edited from 1908 to 1931 by the poet, author, journalist and reformist Mary Gilmore (1865–1962). Over the years, she received hundreds of recipes from all over Australia and New Zealand, many of which she collected into *The Worker Cook Book*, first published in 1915. The contributions were said to have been 'mainly the every-day recipes of Australian housekeepers in working-class homes'—though some of them were probably a bit better than ordinary.

COOKERY BOOKS

... did [your mother] have a cookery book?

—No. No. *[Laughing.]*

Did you ever have any cookery books? ... where did you get your recipes from?

—Out of your head. You didn't have any. I never used recipes.

Did you ever hear of 'Mrs Beeton's Cookery Book'?

—I suppose I saw it around somewhere. I don't remember.

What about the 'Ladies' Home Journal'?

—No, I didn't have any.

The 'New Idea'?

—No, they were not in existence.

—A.D., b.1890

When 'well-educated' mistresses had to turn cook and do for themselves and their families, it was fairly natural for them to look to written instructions. In the early decades of the twentieth century, the conditions were right for increased production of Australian cookery books: the extended education of schoolgirls in the culinary art, the existence of a vast store of practical knowledge and experience to be shared, a new class of highly literate cooks on the look-out for recipes, falling printing and distribution costs, and the rapid growth of advertising for food and domestic products—all contributed to the boom. Most printed cookery books fell into one of four broad classes.

First, there were the textbooks for school, college or commercial cookery courses, some of which have already been mentioned.

A second class of text, taking hold in the first decades of the twentieth century, arose out of the newspapers and journals. Some time in the 1890s, 'Rita' of the *Melbourne Herald* produced a booklet titled *Cottage Cookery*; and in 1900 Zara Aronson (who edited the *Sydney Mail*'s women's pages and contributed to several others) offered *XXth Century Cookery and Home Decoration*. Another writer, Henrietta Walker (née McGowan), was described by the Melbourne newspapers as one of the pioneers of women's journalism; her work included the *Keeyuga Cookery Book* of 1911. *The Worker Cook Book* has already been mentioned. In 1927 a Melbourne weekly, the *Leader*, likewise instituted a 'Spare Corner' column in which women were encouraged to share recipes and household hints: it proved so popular that the best contributions were gathered into a series of booklets published in several forms over many subsequent years.

In the late 1930s arrived two interesting books sponsored by women's magazines: the *Woman's Mirror Cookery Book* and *Woman's Tested Recipes*. And within another decade or two there came possibly the most influential of all series of cookery books: those produced by the *Australian Women's Weekly*. The *Weekly*'s illustrated booklets, with such titles as *Family Dinners* and *Cookery for Parties,* presented prize-winning recipes from competitions. Then came a parade of full-scale cookery books, the first of which were British, adapted for Australia. Although many of the dishes were familiar (though the symbolic Anzac biscuits and lamingtons were both missing), and there were plenty of salads, the overall impression was 'cool climate', and the presentation distinctly English.

The layout of cookery books, too, had come a long way since Hannah Glasse. In terms of text, it was now common (at least in the quality books) to list all the ingredients at the beginning of a recipe and to try to describe the whole method for making the dish in a logical order. Cooking times and oven temperatures were usually given (though as a guide only, for in practice they varied greatly from stove to stove). In terms of illustration, still fairly uncommon in cookery books, these new works also took a lead. *The Australian Women's Weekly Picture Cookery* book explained it this way:

> Primarily we have tried to present in *Picture Cookery* a colourful and interesting book that will be beautiful to look at and easy to use. In the belief that pictures tell the story better than words, the recipes and instructions have been kept as short and concise as possible, so that the busy cook-housewife may be encouraged to experiment with new ideas and methods in the certainty that they can be easily carried out, and that the result will be a well-cooked dish which her family will enjoy.

A *Women's Weekly* cooking supplement from 1946, and its *Family Dinners* booklet, featuring prize recipes from a cooking competition

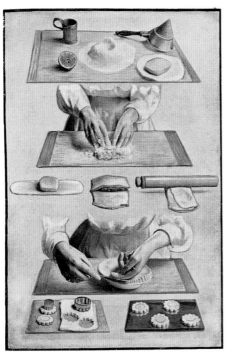

This work was lavishly illustrated with black-and-white photographs and two dozen full-page colour plates, and was to set the pattern for future popular cookery books: large format, a riot of colour, an enticing array of new ideas and old faithfuls rejuvenated, and recipes designed to take the risk out of cooking.

PRODUCT PROMOTION BOOKS

A third kind of cookery book was that put out to promote products or services. As early as 1872 a collection of *Recipes for Cooking Australian Meat* was published to help the canned meat industry which had begun exporting to Britain in the late 1860s. And in 1892, Harriet Wicken had produced *Fish Dainties* to promote sales of the refrigerated product in Melbourne. The concept of such works was a good one: by providing a few recipes, companies could break down the barrier of customer unfamiliarity with their product and ensure that the cook's first experience with it was a success. This was also a good way of showing how to substitute the new product for something already in use.

It was not long before Australians were being offered free recipes from every direction. Some were just small pamphlets presenting a few dishes for a single product or brand of products, as exemplified by a 1909 newspaper advertisement promising that 'twelve pint Blanc-Manges can be made with a pound of the best Corn Flour—Wade's!' (The Wade promotion went on to explain that many 'cheap' cornflours would not make nearly as much; moreover 'their flavour bears no comparison with Wade's'. A book of '46 recipes for dainty dishes, and fish and vegetable sauces' could be had by sending a penny stamp to the agents.)

A few such works more transparently used the recipes as mere token vehicles for advertising. (In 1936, for instance, the manufacturers of Dr Morse's Indian Root Pills, a very heavily advertised patent medicine—actually a laxative—circulated a cheap booklet under the label *Please Retain for I Contain Cooking Recipes and Health Hints*—but the booklet contained rather more advertising material than cooking advice.) While some booklets were plain and cheap, others were attractively produced, with colourful covers. The better ones were offered for sale, though many may have been given free to valued customers. The *Davis Dainty Dishes* books, for instance—first issued in 1922—made generous use of colour (and, incidentally, promoted a jellied pudding which it called 'Pavlova', about the time that Herbert Sachse invented the famous meringue confection known by the same name). Other popular booklets promoting brand-names were produced by White Wings flour, Aerophos raising agent, Willow cookware and many others.

Marketing boards also made good use of promotional recipe booklets. Naturally, they emphasised versatility. *Milk and Cream in Cooking*, for example, showed how the products could be used in soups, fish, meat and poultry dishes, as well as puddings and cakes. And *About Australian Honey* (1965) found a place for the product in traditional dishes such as fruit cakes, mince pies, lamingtons and bread and butter pudding—while also suggesting some Asian-style meat dishes which could be made with honey. (It would be interesting to know how many people tried the recipe for honey and cheese grilled on toast.)

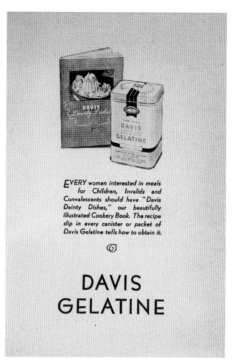

Dainty Dishes
A book of Selected Recipes by NESTLÉ'S

EVERY woman interested in meals for Children, Invalids and Convalescents should have "Davis Dainty Dishes," our beautifully illustrated Cookery Book. The recipe slip in every canister or packet of Davis Gelatine tells how to obtain it.

DAVIS GELATINE

Product promotion booklets and pamphlets. Nestlé's *Dainty Dishes*, and a recipe from one of the many Davis Gelatine booklets

Among the most important sources of recipe books have been the manufacturers of gas and electric cooking appliances and the suppliers of gas and electricity. Their publications were mainly designed to show how familiar and favourite dishes could be made with the new fuels and cooking appliances, or how new and exciting dishes could be added to the repertoire. (Even today, very few new kitchen appliances are offered for sale without some kind of accompanying recipe book.) Many of these works were complete cookery books, sold separately, and remained useful kitchen handbooks long after the cook had become quite comfortable with the operating techniques of the new appliance.

A problem for the early gas cookery books was that the stoves did not all have the same method of temperature control—those put out by the gas companies were able to add little to the directions that could be found in any general cookery book. They were popular nonetheless, including such examples as *Cookery Class Recipes* (by Isabel Ross of Melbourne's Metropolitan Gas Company; 1900), *Gas Cookery* (by Eugenie Ludlow of the Brisbane Gas Company; 1939) and the books of Annie Sharman of the South Australian Gas Company. Brand-name manuals were able to be more specific about temperature control: the book for Parkinson stoves (Victoria) gave its 'adjusto' settings; and the Radiation books (British, but widely sold here) had their own 'regulo' ones.

The battle between gas and electric cooking was also fought out in the books. Among the champions of electricity were Violet McKenzie of the Electrical Association for Women, whose cookery book first came out in 1936, promising that 'an all electric kitchen means freedom' and that 'cooking electrically means complete confidence and a higher standard of living'. However, this confidence probably didn't come just by buying an electric stove: automatic temperature control was rare. A good oven had two heating elements: top and bottom, each of which could be set to high, medium or low. Temperature control was achieved by varying these settings and the position of the food: a joint of meat, for example, would be placed on a low shelf and the top element turned off after the meat had started to brown. When the meat was

SHEEPS' TONGUE SHAPES

Boil 3 tongues until tender; skin and slice thinly. Arrange in a mould or cake tin. Fill mould with slices. Dissolve 2 dessert spoons (half ounce) of Davis gelatine in 2 cups (1 pint) hot stock (water flavoured with meat or vegetable extract); add salt, pepper and nutmeg. When cool, strain over tongues and leave to set. Serve garnished with shredded lettuce, sliced tomato and parsley. If liked, the stock may be flavoured by adding three cloves, one bay leaf, slices of onion, pinch of curry powder, in addition to ingredients mentioned.

—Davis Gelatine recipe booklet

Their dream home must have a Modern Kitchen...
equipped with ... GAS of course!

The easy-to-keep house of today — and tomorrow — has a Modern Kitchen that runs automatically . . . by Gas of course. The 4 Big Domestic Jobs — Cooking, Hot Water, Refrigeration and Heating — are done with unique efficiency and reliability by Gas.

It's smart . . . it's modern to equip your New Home with Gas. Remember, for added leisure and more time for pleasure . . . insist on Gas.

Select approved appliances at your Gas Company Showrooms.

GAS
FOR THE 4 BIG JOBS

COOKING . . HOT WATER . . REFRIGERATION . . HEATING

INSERTED BY THE NATIONAL GAS ASSOCIATION OF AUSTRALIA

Pressure Cooker Recipes

Price 5/6

The modern gas kitchen, in a 1946 issue of *The Australian Women's Weekly*; and a pressure cooker recipe booklet advocating the device's utility for a diverse range of soups, fish, meats, savouries, vegetables, puddings, sauces, cereals and jams (Sydney: Wm Scotow, 1949)

half-cooked, the pudding could be placed in the oven—under the meat if it needed a high temperature, or above (shielded from the bottom element) if it needed a lower temperature. A thermometer fitted to the oven door gave at best only a general idea of what was going on inside. Thermostatic controls marked in degrees of temperature seemed to promise simpler oven management than 'regulos' and 'adjustos'—though electric cooks still knew that every oven was different and had to be approached on its own terms.

This flood of promotional books and pamphlets—covering almost every area of cookery—helped shape Australian food culture. The works have subtly, and sometimes not-so-subtly, influenced both our choice of ingredients (more honey, more milk or cream, more dried fruits—always at the expense of something else) and our cookery techniques (e.g. more frying, less baking; more by microwave, less by steaming). They have certainly influenced the amount of time we are prepared to spend in the kitchen.

THE PEOPLE'S RECIPES: FUNDRAISING AND CHARITY BOOKS

The fourth class of cookery books to proliferate this century has been those belonging to the people. Whatever the teachers have said may be good or proper, whatever the journalists have said may be interesting or fashionable, and whatever the manufacturers might have told us about new devices and techniques might or might not be persuasive—but the people themselves have always been ready to say what recipes they think are, or are not, worth passing on.

In Australia it all probably started with the Presbyterian Church in Queensland, whose Women's Missionary Union produced a small cookery book in 1894. The New South Wales women followed in 1895, with a work bearing the charming title *Cookery Book of Good and Tried Receipts*, first offered at a 'grand Sale of Work and Missionary Exhibition' in Sydney. This book was a rather important contribution to Australia's food history for several reasons. First, it was only ever concerned with the plain cookery of ordinary households (the recipes were contributed by the women themselves, so it truly was a people's book); from 1896 until 1979 the Women's Missionary Association kept revising the book, deleting recipes that had passed out of favour, and adding new ones. Second, it is probably the longest-running Australian cookery book. And third, its slightly conservative approach to cookery meant that it acted as a recorder of already-accepted ideas among Australian cooks, rather than as a promoter of new ones.

It was not long before other contributor books appeared, to raise funds for church or charity. The *Goulburn Cookery Book* and the Country Women's Association books have been mentioned. Other well-known works, especially to earlier generations of Australian cooks, are the *Green and Gold Cookery Book* (a fundraiser for the King's College, Adelaide), the *Kookaburra Cookery Book* (for the Lady Victoria Buxton Girl's Club, South Australia), and the *Hobart Cookery Book* (originally for the Methodist Central Mission, Hobart). Branches of the Red Cross have also produced popular cookery books. And the two World Wars have brought many small fundraisers, probably assembled from contributed recipes: the *War Chest Cookery Book*, a series of little booklets put out by the Disabled Men's Association, and Annie King's *'Carry On' Cookery Book* are examples. In fact, charity inspired what might have been Western Australia's answer to Mrs Beeton's monumental work, had the public taken to it: *The Australian Household Guide* was on a similar scale—400 pages of household advice, followed by more than 700 pages of recipes. It was edited in 1916 by Lady Deborah Hackett. (When the Second World War began, she produced a second edition of the volume for the Red Cross.)

There can hardly be a church, charity or community organisation (school, interest group, sporting association) that has not at some time rallied its members to a fundraising cause and put together a cookery book. Very many of them are circulated informally—sold to the members who contributed the recipes, to their friends and a few supporters. Unless they are formally published, they may never make it into a permanent public collection. Yet for the scholar willing to tackle the problems of identification, dating and cataloguing, these works may provide one of the most authentic accounts of the popular culture of the Australian kitchen.

The *War Chest Cookery Book*
(Sydney: Websdale Shoosmith, 1917)

UPS AND DOWNS

After repeated crop failures and near-starvation in its early years, economic prospects in the colony gradually began to brighten. Completion of a road across the Blue Mountains in 1815 opened up the western slopes and plains, and the wool industry boomed. Although Australia felt the effect of economic depression in Europe in the 1840s, the country was buoyed by the gold discoveries of 1851 and the resultant flood of fortune-hunters pouring into the country. Gold, wool—and, later, grain, meat and dairy—sustained generally good times up until the First World War (though broken by a period of severe depression in the late 1880s). The Great Depression of the 1930s stamped its memory indelibly on those who lived through it—with a renewed belief in the virtue of economy and 'sustainable' growth. The Second World War brought more restrictions, followed by more good times in the 1950s and 1960s, and further fluctuations up to the present time.

Changes in economic fortune are usually reflected in the way Australians eat. When times are looking up—towards higher incomes, or lower prices and taxes—we feel expansive, and it isn't hard to find ways of eating better. And, of course, the shop-keepers and eating houses are always there, eager to help us celebrate prosperity or good fortune. In the kitchen, we might begin to think that it was time to try artichokes; that a goose or hare was hardly an extravagance, or that a dish of fresh figs would be an appetising idea.

In the early nineteenth century, just having enough to eat was itself prosperity—while a better class of tea, a York ham, some bottled fruits and sauces, and best dried fruits for the Christmas pudding were luxuries. A hundred years ago we could have turned to *Mrs Maclurcan's Cookery Book* and found there a recipe for roast turkey 'for special menus'—quite special indeed, with *pâté de foie gras* stuffing and truffle garnish. For the cabinet pudding,

(above) Edward Roper (c.1830–1904)
Christmas Dinner at the Diggings c.1855
oil on canvas on cardboard; 19 x 12.2 cm
From the Pictorial Collection

(right) A productive pioneer's garden around 1900
[*Bush hut, Gippsland, Victoria*]
Photograph by Nicholas Caire (1837–1918)
20.7 x 27.7 cm
In: *Victorian Views.* [Melbourne] Manufactured by
Sands & McDougall for Department of Agriculture,
1900.
From the Pictorial Collection

(below) This advertised ham would definitely have been viewed as a 'luxury' by many Australian householders of the time—and is often still a special Christmas indulgence

PINEAPPLE
BACON & HAMS
HUTTON'S
FLAVOUR DELICIOUS
QUALITY UNAPPROACHABLE
PINE-APPLE
HAMS.

we might have followed Isabel Ross (*Cookery Class Recipes*, 1900): Genoise cake and macaroons drizzled with brandy or liqueur, steeped in rich egg yolk custard, lavishly decorated with crystallised cherries and glacé fruit, and steamed in a decorative mould. Half a century later, in the 1950s, housewives only had to look to the *Women's Weekly* which in its regular column, 'Today's Luxury Dish', offered such suggestions as lobster figaro. Now, at the end of the twentieth century, anyone wanting to spend money on food is tempted from every side.

Bad times, on the contrary, bring unemployment, or static incomes and high prices: the economy of the roast gives way to economy all round. Hard times call for strict control of kitchen expenses, more inventiveness and adaptability. In the land which had been famous for workers having meat three times a day, even that commodity could be too expensive.

From the earliest times, the books gave recipes for economical cookery—cakes made without butter or eggs, puddings with very little fruit, and so on. There were recipes such as 'cheap soup for the poor' or 'cheap family white soup'. This was a continuous theme, for even in the best of times there could be a place for economy. Cookery books continued to offer economical versions of dishes that might have been better, the women's magazines occasionally ran features on economical cooking, and there has always been a market for whole books devoted to economy.

The recession years of the early 1890s introduced into the cookery books such dishes as poor man's goose (made of sheep heart and liver, potatoes, onions and sage) and vegetable goose (which was, in effect, the stuffing without a goose around it). The humble cottage pie would be topped with pastry made with dripping instead of butter—or, often, just with mashed potatoes. During the First World War, good meat was so expensive that women's columns in the newspapers urged even middle-class housewives to turn to rabbit and to fish (especially the cheaper, deep-sea varieties). The columnists frequently gave recipes for making the most of 'economical cuts'. The *Sydney Morning Herald* of 16 June 1915 put it this way:

> The family dinner of soup, a joint, and pudding, with plenty of eggs and butter, must [now] be superseded by something else, must suffer a change into 'something' not necessarily 'rich,' but very decidedly 'strange.' The men of the family are the sufferers. Their meals are very important to them; and when a man accustomed to a nice sirloin is offered, say, a sheep's head broth, with the skull to follow, he is apt to look a trifle more gloomy and depressed than the war news has already made him. Still, sheep's head broth makes a satisfying dish.

> The broth, made with pearl barley, a minced onion, carrot and turnip, spring onions or leeks, and a sprig of parsley, may be served first. (It should be simmered for two hours.) Then the head, if the spectacle be not regarded as too gruesome, should be sprinkled with bread crumbs, and browned in the oven. The brains should have been cooked separately, and made into a sauce with milk, flour and butter, or they may be turned into balls with the minced tongue and fried. The Scottish way is to cut off pieces of the flesh from the head and serve it in the tureen with the broth, and this may be recommended in preference to the rather ghoulish plan of serving up the 'tete coupee.'

(It is interesting to note in passing that the writer of this piece, a woman, saw the Australian addiction to meat as a male thing.)

The Second World War brought many such 'gruesome' dishes back again, helped by such publications as *Planning Meat Ration Meals* and *War-time Cookery*.

RABBITING

... when there was no other work the men went rabbiting [for] skins—you could make quite a good living then, and apart from that they were good food. A lot of people lived on them in the Depression years. Killed the rabbits, ate the rabbits, sold the skins. It was the only means they had ... We had our share. I loved it ... Bake them or boil them ... stew. Whatever way ... You used to get a bit sick of them sometimes ... —N.B., b.1899

BROILED RABBIT

Take a young rabbit and open it right down; remove the head and wash well in salted water. Dry the carcase, flatten it out and season lightly with salt and freshly ground black pepper, rub all over with butter, and broil over a clear fire for about 35 or 40 minutes. A little green butter may be put over it when serving.
(To 'green' butter mix it with parsley or spinach juice.)

—Mary Gilmore (ed.), *The Worker Cook Book*, 1915

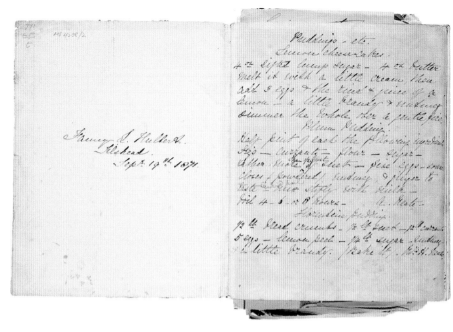

COOKING WITH GRANDMA

Jackie French

Grandma's memories always harkened back to food—like the time she was shipwrecked somewhere on the New South Wales coast when she was four and they wandered for days, till they came upon a farm where the woman made scones and scones and scones because she ran out of bread, and there was plum jam and peach jam and prickly pear jam which Grandma had never tasted before. I spent most of the holidays of my childhood with my grandmother. I can't remember us doing much except eating, but that always seemed enough. Cooking food, setting the table or clearing it away; shopping for food or driving somewhere to eat it or the occasional expedition (they were always 'expeditions' with Grandma) to eat scones and jam and cream, or buy fresh fish or oranges or have picnics by the waves.

I have Grandma's recipe book next to me as I write—orange soufflé (the recipe sent by a Miss Gibbs) and eggless banana cake (at the bottom of a letter from her sister-in-law in World War Two) and creamed tapioca from her aunt. It was from Grandma I learnt that the fabric of life should be good; that paradise is made up of the million small things that fill your day; and if you want an index to the life that someone leads, just look at the food they eat.

What you eat, of course, depends on the choices you have made about your life. If you choose to work in an office from 9 am till who knows when, you'll live on food cooked by other people, or on what you can scavenge from supermarket shelves after it's been shipped, washed, packaged, processed ... I'm not saying you can't eat well, but you probably won't, unless you've been dreaming about food in the hours you should have been working.

(top) A household notebook kept in two volumes by Fanny Hulbert, from around 1871. Typical of these works, it collects such diverse items as home cures for rheumatism and diarrhoea, instructions for the production of fumigating powder, and patterns for knitting sox. Also typical of such scrapbooks still kept by householders today, it is stuffed with cut-out recipes from newspapers and loose inserts from friends and acquaintances—such as this beautifully handscripted recipe *(above)* for 'orange brandy or gin' Rex Nan Kivell Collection; from the Manuscript Collection

(right) Jackie French in 1992
Photograph by Virginia Wallace-Crabbe
gelatin-silver photograph; 25.4 x 20.2 cm
From the Pictorial Collection

A gentler era, perhaps offering more time for the shared appreciation of good, simple food
Louisa Haynes (1863–1956)
Bush Picnic Scene near Adelaide 1896
oil on canvas; 17.8 x 25.3 cm
From the Pictorial Collection

Food is becoming a smaller and smaller part of our lives. Most of the kitchens I've been in lately just don't *have* any food—not open packets of flour and half-empty canisters of brown sugar and bottles of vanilla essence. They've got cereal in the cupboard and yoghurt and chicken breasts in the fridge, with maybe three oranges and a carton of milk and a Gladwrapped tin of cat food that's stinking out the kitchen, but the owner doesn't notice because that's what kitchens smell like these days ... just like they don't notice the taste of artificial vanilla and preservatives in the fruit cakes, 'hot bake' biscuits, plum puddings, commercial Christmas shortbreads—food that is disgusting unless your tastebuds know nothing else.

Food in my childhood was a ritual, even with my mother, who couldn't cook. (Given that my mother tackles everything else life throws at her with joy and gusto, I suspect her lack of cooking ability was a subconscious defence against the life she didn't want to lead but which was the only one available to her in the 1950s.)

It's a ritual that still exists to a limited extent in country New South Wales, where I live now. (It's no coincidence I choose to live my life where food—the growing of it, the cooking of it, the eating, is still central to many people's lives.) It is unfriendly not to offer food as soon as someone arrives at your door; reprehensible not to preserve/transform the seasonal surpluses of fruit, tomatoes, eggs, and to offer recent vintages of jams, pickles, chutneys to the next few days of callers. It is your duty to send plates and casseroles to the sick or bereaved; to invite strangers to a meal, and friends to celebrate. But these customs are dying too.

Like Grandma, I remember my life in images of its food—the burnt chops and lumpy mashed potato of my childhood, cooked with anguish, eaten with despair; the 10 001 things to do with soya beans and the pumpkins handed to us over the fence from my student days ... and then the richer years, as I lived where food was grown as well as eaten. The years on the avocado orchard, still with a student budget, which meant avocado mousse, salad, cheesecake, stuffing, soup, soufflé (you need to add pistachios, as avocado loses its flavour when it's cooked). The years living in a shed, where I cooked on a two-burner kerosene stove, till one grass-shrivelling day it blew up. (Luckily I'd dashed out to pick some carrots.)

JACKIE FRENCH'S ARALUEN APHIDS, AU NATUREL

Choose aphids that are feeding on something edible—roses, say, or cabbages. (And bushes that haven't been sprayed.) Scrape off with your finger nail. Crunch with your front teeth, so the sweetness shivers along your tongue.

Those were the adventurous years, when I discovered that aphids taste good (but don't try them if they're feeding on something toxic) and emu berries vary from bush to bush (i.e. from yummy cardboard flavour, to bitter) and that home-grown snails are just as good as the ones in tins (i.e. both are chewy and completely tasteless, unless you cook them thoroughly and add garlic butter).

Why was it, during those years, that I met so many people who were eager to show me the—shall we say less travelled by-paths of Australian cooking? Why you should hang a wombat (it's tough until it begins to melt off the bone); how to track a pigeon, and why Indian Game are the best eating birds in cultivated fowldom; the pleasures of green ant juice, and how to cook dinner in a pumpkin in the ashes, or make hearth cakes on a granite boulder, or cook an egg on the roof of the Land Rover, or yabbies in a rock pool.

A few of those recipes have lingered—I still cook grass-seed hearth-cakes, when I can be bothered with the picking, and make thorn bush 'pesto', and last year's Christmas cake was flavoured with grevillea and roses.

Even if most people in Australia eat poorly, this is still a golden age of food. If you want to (and the emphasis is still on *if*) it is possible to eat extraordinarily well, with fresh food unthought of in Grandma's day, cooking techniques, appliances and recipes from all around the world. It's not the raw ingredients that are lacking today; or the knowledge. It's the time—time to savour the cuppa and Sao biscuits for 'early morning tea', time to natter as you peel and slice your peach at breakfast, time to mooch around the garden gathering this and that, and putting them together so they form a meal.

A life that doesn't have time for food—and the rituals and conversations associated with food—is empty. It's lost its soul, its savour and its rhythms.

That's what I learned from Grandma.

GRANDMA'S STUFFED SHOULDER OF LAMB

You can't buy shoulders for stuffing anymore. They're boned and rolled, and they should be hogget anyway—the sheep equivalent of a teenager. Grandma spent a decade trying to maintain her supply while increasingly depending on others to shop for her, then turned to leg of lamb instead. But it wasn't the same. Finish the following with stewed peaches and baked custard and a strong cup of tea. And raise a toast to Grandma.

If you want to attempt a roast shoulder, find a butcher who sells sides of lamb. Explain carefully you don't want the shoulder boned. Make a long, deep pocket across the base of the shoulder. (I know this sounds vague but once you get the knife in one hand and the meat in the other you'll see what I mean.)

Mix breadcrumbs, chopped onion, fresh thyme, sage, grated lemon zest, melted butter (not low cholesterol—none of Grandma's diet was). Stuff mixture into shoulder.

Roast the stuffed meat with a branch of rosemary slowly for at least three hours. Dripping's optional. Add spuds and pumpkin (their caramelised residue makes the gravy sweet) as soon as there's hot fat. (If it isn't hot, they'll turn soft, not crispy.) Turn every hour.

When the meat's so tender it shreds rather than slices (the French would hate it—not a hint of pink, but if the meat really is hogget, and it's slowly cooked, a grey roast is just as good as pink—just a different meal entirely) and the veg are black and caramelised at the sides, hoik the whole lot onto a plate in the oven while you make the gravy.

I'm not going to even try to explain how to make gravy—it's something you have to watch, the delicate browning of the flour and the cooking, cooking, cooking till you get something other than brown glue. If you can't make gravy already—and don't have a Grandma to show you how—skim off the fat, add good red wine to the juices, boil severely for a few minutes, then use that instead.

IMPORTING COOKS

THE IMPACT OF MIGRATION

We have seen how modern Australian food and cooking were built on traditions imported from Britain, rather than on those of the Aboriginal people, and how those imported traditions were adapted to suit local conditions. It would be wrong, however, to dismiss early Australian cookery as merely or mostly British.

First, the British influence was in fact predominantly *English*. (The second largest group of newcomers was the Irish, though very little of them can be seen in the cookery books—even the famous Irish stew probably came via England, where it was already established; coming from generally poor backgrounds, the Irish did more to entrench the meat-damper-tea routine than to extend the range of kitchen cookery. The third largest group was the Scots: they included many who were quite well-to-do, or soon became so in Australia, and their influence is easily found in our early books.) Second, the cookery of England was not merely 'English', but had already absorbed many culinary ideas from its neighbours, competitors and imperial territories. The Indian 'curries', Italian pasta ('macaroni'), German yeast cookery and the many dishes copied from France are just a few of the more obvious examples to be found in the Australian cookery books.

The rough table experienced en route may not necessarily have improved on arrival
C.J. Stanliland (1838–1916)
Emigrants Going to Australia
hand-coloured wood engraving; 31.5 x 46 cm
From the Pictorial Collection

(below) Antipodes-bound emigrants James Mackay and family sailed from Scotland in 1845. Fowls are depicted among the hand luggage
Elizabeth Walker (1800–76), after W. Alsworth
The Emigrants
hand-coloured lithograph; 45.2 x 57.2 cm
Rex Nan Kivell Collection; from the Pictorial Collection

Australians were also open to new ideas arriving directly from overseas. An influence beginning in the late 1830s was the large numbers of German emigrants coming to South Australia. Many formed rural communities at Hahndorf and the Barossa Valley, where they preserved much of the culture of their homeland. This makes the *Barossa Cookery Book*, which dates to 1917, particularly interesting: leafing through it, we find a parade of German names among the contributors, and a few specialties such as *honig kuchen*—but remarkably few recipes that could not be found in several other Australian books of the period. (A notable exception is perhaps the several recipes for our famous Sao biscuit.) Many other cookery book compilers already reflected the German influence in such dishes as sauerkraut, dumplings, bread puddings, pickled red cabbage and yeast cookery.

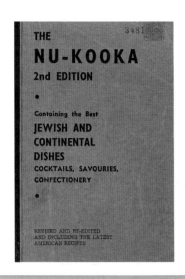

THE
NU-KOOKA
2nd EDITION

•

Containing the Best
JEWISH AND
CONTINENTAL
DISHES
COCKTAILS, SAVOURIES,
CONFECTIONERY

•

REVISED AND RE-EDITED
AND INCLUDING THE LATEST
AMERICAN RECIPES

MATZO KLISE NO 2

Soak 2 matzos in water until
soft, then squeeze dry as
possible. Fry in 2 tablespoons
of chicken fat, adding
1 tablespoon chopped onion,
a little pepper, 1/2 teaspoonful
ginger, 1 1/2 teaspoons salt,
1 tablespoon chopped parsley,
and 1 cup matzo meal whilst
matzos are hot. Remove to a
bowl and when cool add
4 eggs, beating them in one at
a time. Form balls, roll in
matzo meal and chicken fat,
and boil 20 minutes in soup.

—The Nu-Kooka

A Greek family celebrates Easter Day 1975 with a
spitted lamb in their Melbourne backyard
Photograph by John McKinnon; Australian
Information Service
From the Pictorial Collection

Another early ethnic influence came from journalist Zara Aronson, born of Jewish parents and educated in England, Germany and Sydney. Through her newspaper columns from the 1890s, and her cookery books, she introduced many readers to a wider range of German and Jewish dishes. Jewish cookery had in fact made a very early appearance in Australian food literature: Edward Abbott included a collection of Hebrew recipes in the first local cookery book back in 1864; and they were reissued in 1867 in a separate pamphlet. (A much later example is the Australian Jewish community's publication of *The Nu-Kooka* book as a fundraiser in the 1940s.)

Likewise, many American recipes found their way to Australia—and still do.

CONTINENTAL COOKERY

What of the other countries whose cookery had been represented in the *Woman* and *Woman's Mirror* magazines? The curiosity shown by Australian food writers at the beginning of the twentieth century about 'foreign food' had been soon eclipsed by other concerns. The First World War had kindled strong national and imperial sentiments: it was a good time to cook British. Wartime austerities also made it a time to cook economically. The novelty of foreign food was largely put aside in favour of the half-forgotten recipes for cheap living—which, of course, were British. As the *Sydney Morning Herald* of 16 June 1915 commented:

> Many old-fashioned recipes are being dug up from memories of 'what grandmother did', or perchance from an old family cookery book in MS. [manuscript], treasured no less for its directions than for its quaint wording. We are finding that a war-time dietary must exclude much of what we have until quite recently regarded as necessaries.

At the end of the war, national sentiment remained fixed on the empire. The pre-war schemes for encouraging British migration were revived, and kept Australia's population topped up with new arrivals expecting to cook and eat British food. The flow, however, was not all from Britain. From as early as the gold rush days there had been small, but significant migrations from other countries, especially Scandinavia. By 1891, about one in ten of Australian residents born overseas had come from outside the British Isles. Italians came to the Victorian gold fields in the 1850s, to Queensland in the 1860s and to Sydney in the 1880s; more came in the early nineteenth century, and by 1939 large numbers of Italian-born people had settled here. Many newcomers also came from Greece and from other areas of Europe prior to World War Two.

The food traditions of non-British communities within Australia were again making their presence felt. The wartime eclipse was passing, and by the late 1930s interest in foreign food had been rekindled—this time as 'Continental cookery'. The change was demonstrated by the Cosmopolitan Publishing Company of Melbourne bringing out what, its title claimed, was *The First Australian Continental Cookery Book*, 'printed in Australia for Australians'. With no named author, the book's bold aim was 'to flash a ray or two of light into the occasionally somewhat obscure recesses of traditional British cookery'. The work was a fascinating mixture. Some of the recipes were English favourites, with or without a 'continental' twist. Others, such as fennel sprouts (bulbs) in butter, were novel. *Macedoine à la Kosciusko* was certainly a novel dish: a mini-mountain of 'fresh snow' and fruit macerated in liqueur. (The recipe allowed that 'If you are not on Mount Kosciusko and have no snow, you can make the best of it with some broken ice.') The book featured many Italian specialties, such as fried large calamaries and *zabaione*, and a no-frills approach to pizza, given in the chapter on 'savouries'.

For Australia, the Second World War did not end so much in a flush of imperial sentiment, like the first—but in a growing realisation that the nation would have to make its own way in the world. Increased population growth seemed the answer—or a large part of it—and once again immigration programs were swung into action. Although British migrants were again preferred, many others came too. More than two million new settlers arrived between 1947 and 1969: 12 per cent of them from non-British northern Europe; 15 per cent from central Europe; and 25 per cent from southern Europe.

British arrivals aboard the *Fairsea*,
Sydney Harbour, 1968
Photograph by Douglas Baglin; Department of Immigration
From the Pictorial Collection

After five years here, one of these newcomers—Janos Gelencser—produced *The Continental Flavour* (195–) designed to gently introduce Australians to European dishes they could make at home or order confidently from a hotel or restaurant menu. Some of the dishes (such as lobster chow min) and some of the names (*lamb's fry au onions*) were not very continental. *Braised fowl à la English* was neither. The book devoted more than half a page to explaining what a frankfurter is and what to do with it, and described 20 or so other meat products sold as 'smallgoods'. While not pretending that Australians could enjoy the traditional and famous game dishes of Europe, it gave a few ideas for local possibilities: wild duck, hare, rabbit, pheasant, kangaroo tail and kangaroo joey. (That last suggestion was certainly ignored.)

Again, the newspapers and magazines of the day helped stimulate interest among food-minded non-Europeans. Maria Kozslik Donovan's *Continental Cookery in Australia* (1955) brought together French, Italian, Viennese, Hungarian and other continental recipes which had appeared in the Melbourne *Age* and *Sun*. The *Women's Weekly* featured Danish, French and other cuisines.

By 1970, the large and colourful cookery books being promoted by women's magazines routinely included recipes for many international dishes.

THE MELTING-POT

As a result of all these influences, Australia's menu at the end of the twentieth century has a complex identity. As cultures interact, it is becoming harder to describe Australian food in terms of ethnic origins. Already, some prefer to think of our kitchen as a global melting-pot. Whether the delightfully distinctive components will retain their ethnic authenticity, meld into some new chop suey, or gradually become Australianised like the curries of old India, is a question food-lovers can only ponder.

The answer does not lie with them—but with the manufacturers and merchants.

AN IMMIGRANT

[After] they killed a bullock or a sheep ... it amused me to see them hang the meat out on top of a tree and put a chaff bag round it or have a barrel to salt it down. —N.B., b.1899

A NEAPOLITAN RECIPE

There have been worse recipes for pizza since this one; it has on occasion been made with ready-mix scone dough.

You require some leavened bread-dough. You can make it at home with some brewer's yeast. Spread it out with a rolling-pin until it is an inch thick. Then grease a pie-dish, place the dough in it, making a border for it round the rim. Scatter over the top three or four tomatoes (peeled and cut into pieces), and finally put over them a third of a pound of rather fresh cheese cut into slices. Put into the oven until the dough is well cooked.

—*The First Australian Continental Cookery Book*

THE GREEK CAFF

James Castrission was born in Kythera, Greece, in 1902. He migrated to Australia in 1914, and later bought a café with his uncle in Gundagai, New South Wales. As well as meals, light refreshments and sandwiches, the café had a milk bar and sold smallgoods, fruit and vegetables.

... there were ... Australian cafés [in Gundagai] ... in a small way—but they couldn't compare or compete against us because we used to work too hard and used to give them their money's worth and we used to give them good meals, nice steak-and-eggs and whatever they wanted for a fair price—and we not only had meals, we had sandwiches and light refreshments and we stocked smallgoods ...

... we stocked fruit and vegetables, and there was a milkbar there ... we gave them quality and the price was right and everything that we sold to them it was good quality, whatever they buy, and that's why they came to us ... Say for instance a steak-and-eggs was two and ninepence, we would charge two and ninepence ...

... the average Australian could not compete with us because he used to come to our shop and used to get a lemon squash, beautiful drink, for sixpence. Or other drinks that were nice and cold and tasty and everything— they couldn't compete with us! That's why we did the business!

Frank Hurley (1885–1962)
Greek family milk bar and café in the 1930s (detail)
The eclectic range of names for such establishments
stretches from the likes of the 'California' seen here,
to the more traditionally Hellenic 'Acropolis'
Hurley Collection; from the Pictorial Collection

A CHINESE PUZZLE

One of the interesting questions of Australian food history is why it took us so long to discover Chinese cookery. Shiploads of Southern Chinese, nearly all male, arrived in New South Wales and Victoria in the 1850s. By 1861 there were more than 38 000 of them. Many went to work on the goldfields, where their presence was soon resented by British and Australian-born gold-seekers; cultural and economic tensions developed into outright racial persecution, followed by government measures to stop further migration from Asia.

Many of these Chinese eventually went home; most of those who stayed moved into country towns or the 'Chinatown' communities in Sydney and Melbourne to become merchants, shopkeepers, cabinet-makers, market gardeners and cooks. By the end of the century, 'John Chinaman' was an accepted source of fresh vegetables, and a hotel or station generally did well to employ a Chinese cook (though to produce European-style food!).

But it was another half-century—when the Chinese population had declined to its lowest level since the gold rushes—before Australians took much notice of Chinese food. One of the early signs came in the *'Woman's Mirror' Cookery Book* of 1937, where it was promoted on the strength of health consciousness (a dietary summary was given for each recipe) and popularity (all of its dishes were selected from 'my favourite recipe' contributions over a period of 12 years). In a chapter of 'foreign dishes' this same work gave more than 100 recipes said to have been contributed by 25 'representatives of foreign nations resident in Australia'—including (in addition to China): Czechoslovakia, Denmark, Finland, Greece, Italy, Mexico, Norway, Spain and Sweden.

(above) This menu from Melbourne's Cafe Canton (c.1911) offered an interesting mixed fare (dishes numbered 1–12) of 'turtle soup, woon hoon, edible bird's nest, steamed duck, sweet lotus sweet, chicken and ham, shark's fins, asparagus, French Alaska sweet, dessert, le chec nuts and preserved ginger'
From the Ephemera Collection

(below) S.T. Gill (1818–80)
John Alloo's Chinese Restaurant, Main Road, Ballarat 1853
photolithograph; 11.2 x 19 cm
Rex Nan Kivell Collection; from the Pictorial Collection

Though as far as Chinese cookery is concerned the appearance of these favourites was still before its time. (A couple of years later, *Woman* magazine published a book of recipes selected from a cookery competition and again included dishes from many countries—though none from China.)

An Australian book properly dedicated to Chinese cookery did not appear until 1948. *Cooking the Chinese Way*, by Roy Geechoun, was a modest primer of only 30 recipes, and began with an apologetic introduction to the effect that Australians had 'grown up to the extent that we support in our cities many foreign restaurants, particularly Chinese'—but went on to admit that 'Chinese cooking, like most things Chinese, is a mystery to Australians.'

Six years—and six editions—later it was able to begin a little more confidently: 'Mention Chinese cooking and most of us think of a Chinese café...' By then, change was under way. The magazines had sensed increasing interest among their readers and began to offer recipes for imitating at home the favourite food of the local Chinese takeaway. In 1955 the *Women's Weekly* devoted a cookery feature to 'Food Chinese Style'; and *Woman's Day* put out a Chinese cookery book in 1959. Soon a flood of books came onto the market: Kenneth Lo's *Chinese Food* (1972), Charmaine Solomon's *Chinese Cooking* (1979), Elizabeth Chong's *First Happiness* (1982), and many others.

At the same time, Australian attitudes towards its Asian neighbours more generally were also changing. Trade and travel had increased since the Second World War; the 'White Australia' policy had been dismantled and, from the 1960s, the proportion of Australia's immigrants coming from Asia was growing. By the 1980s Australians had embraced Vietnamese, Indonesian, Japanese, Thai and Korean food. Including at last 'real' Indian: few Australians could now contemplate an old-style curry of cooked meat, onion, apple and curry powder except in wonder.

This pioneering work *(above)* by Roy Geechoun of Melbourne contained 30 popular recipes to 'cook real Chinese meals at home without any difficulty', and was dedicated to 'the furtherance of a greater Australia–Chinese friendship so firmly established during the war years' (Melbourne: W.D. Joynt & Co., 1948)

(right) The Anglo version of the 'Indian curry' was a traditional last resort for disposing of the dregs of the household meat. Here Donald Friend proscribes against even attempting to make a real curry without use of fresh ingredients
From 'Ayam-Ayam Kesayangan' (Donald Friend Diaries)
From the Manuscript Collection

(above right) During and following the gold rushes, many Chinese took up trades as shopkeepers, hawkers or market gardeners
Photograph by R. Rohner
postcard; 14 x 9 cm
Ferguson Collection; from the Pictorial Collection

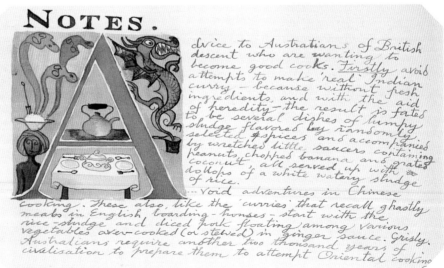

NOTES.

dvice to Australians of British descent who are wanting to become good cooks. Firstly avoid attempts to make 'real' Indian curry – because without fresh ingredients, and with the aid of heredity – the result is fated to be several dishes of lumpy sludge flavored by randomly selected spices and accompanied by wretched little saucers containing peanuts, chopped banana and grated coconut, all served up with dollops of a white watery sludge of rice. ...Void adventures in Chinese cooking. These also, like the 'curries' that recall ghastly meals in English boarding-houses – start with the rice-sludge and diced pork floating among various vegetables over-cooked (or stewed) in ginger sauce. Grisly. Australians require another two thousand years of civilisation to prepare them to attempt Oriental cooking

PATRICK WHITE:
A CULINARY AFICIONADO

I spend half my life at the stove, but fortunately enjoy cooking. It goes with writing.
—letter to Pepe Mamblas, January 1979

Nobel Prize–winning novelist, playwright and short story writer Patrick White (1912–90) was also an aficionado of multicultural cooking, as revealed by his correspondence (*Patrick White Letters*; edited by David Marr; Random House Australia, 1994). The following extracts range, in order, from his 'survival' days at the small property 'Dogwoods' at Castle Hill in Sydney in the 1950s—through his intermittent travels back to Europe, and on to his residency as grand old man of Australian letters at Sydney's Centennial Park.

ON SURVIVAL COOKERY

Australia has become very expensive, even living as we do here. So we grow all the vegetables we can, and yesterday we discovered a dish of garden snails is every bit as good as escargots de Bourgogne. While there are snails and dandelions, obviously one need not starve. —Dogwoods, October 1950

ON BREAD BAKING

If this typing looks unduly peculiar, it is because Tom Jones [the cat] is rolling about on top of the desk, and I am baking a batch of bread at the same time. Lovely smell. I always bake my own bread nowadays. —Dogwoods, April 1957

ON FISH

Apart from the fish, I think we can eat better [back home in Australia] ... But the fish! That is really something, and we have more or less decided to eat nothing else while we are in Greece. To think that Australians believe they know about fish; it is pathetic. Last night we went to a place near the water in Piraeus and feasted with many cousins on clams on the shell, fried baby kalamaria, prawns about six inches long, little red rock cod, of tender, melting flesh (these are perhaps the best of all), and an enormous fish, I don't know what, grilled in the piece, with crisp, salty black and golden skin. All this with plenty of retsina, of course, and raw salads. —Athens, April 1958

ON COOKING AND WRITING

This letter should smell good and garlic-y, as I have been cooking a dish of Imam-Baïldi in between typing. In my middle age I have developed the inconvenient and a-social habit of going to bed after dinner. Then I get up and use the middle and small hours. These are the best for writing letters and cooking, also for revising, though not creating novels; first thing in the morning is best ... for that. — Dogwoods, January 1960

Donald Friend (1914–89)
[Portrait of Patrick White holding *The Tree of Man*]
From 'Ayam-Ayam Kesayangan'
(Donald Friend Diaries)
From the Manuscript Collection

ON AIRLINE FOOD

... just eaten the Qantas dinner—life is a little melancholy. —approaching Athens, October 1963

ON HARES

The reason I am writing so soon is that Maie Casey [wife of Lord Casey, the then Governor-General] was here yesterday ... The lunch turned out very well. The hares arrived two days in advance. After I had cut them up our kitchen was a horrific sight; Duncan's chamber can't have looked bloodier. And the twelve lemons and twenty-four cloves of garlic gave spectacular results. We had chlorophyll for Maie, but she refused to take it. I'm sure those she met later in the day must have suspected the lunch of being a republican plot. —Centennial Park, July 1966

ON THE MEAT PRESS

P.S. You can put any meat in that press provided it has been cooked and boned. It would be good for spiced beef for instance ... I have done things like boiled bacon, pickled pork, and chickens. A whole leg of pork should squeeze into the press you have. It would take a turkey, or goose, or several ducks and chickens. Then when the meat is pressed and cold, you can carve from the slab in professional slices using that [circular knife] you've got, and serve with a glamorous sauce. —Centennial Park, January 1974

ON OMELETTES

Madam Du Val cooked the lunch. Most unwisely they chose to give us omelettes. I went into the kitchen afterward to see her and she said, 'I'm fucked!' She looked it too, after eighty omelettes. I said I was fucked after one; I find cooking an omelette a highly emotional experience. Some of the elderly maids standing around seemed rather shocked. —Centennial Park, April 1975

ON THE SPUD

I was brought up to see the potato as a mortal sin because my mother was a figure fanatic, but in my false-toothy old age it has become one of my great joys. We eat masses of them. —Centennial Park, December 1980

ON MORTALITY AND THE STRUDEL

I went again to the heart man last week, and believe it or not, he wanted me to rush straight to the Prince Henry and have some more electric shocks. I refused because I'd planned to make a strudel stuffed with vegetables and a grüne Sosse [green sauce] at the week-end. I told him I had to have some little frivolity in my life, and this seemed the only way. I think he thought me completely nuts, though I promised to go for the shocks after my visit to the chest expert and my next to the eye surgeon, if I'm still around. —Centennial Park, August 1982

Among other matters in his letter to cousin Peggy Garland (8 October 1975), White comments of a planned overseas trip that 'half the pleasure in travel is, to me, the food', and expresses weariness from a protracted period of cooking for house guests
From the Manuscript Collection
(Reproduced with permission of Barbara Mobbs)

I'm feeling rather exhausted as the result of nearly five months of house-guests, first my youngest niece Frances, now Manoly's sister Elly. Elly is no trouble at all because she is our age, likes the same things, and goes about with us. Frances had to be thought for continually and her reactions to everything are so muted that it is difficult to gather what she likes and thinks. Then there is the cooking. I like that, but towards the end of five months, trying to keep up to scratch cooking for guests and thinking of something different to give them does become a bit of a drag - perhaps nothing to you as you are used to dealing with a large family and a lot of coming and going.

I am becoming old - eyes giving out, teeth crumbling, a feeling of permanent flat exhaustion. Nowadays doctors don't seem able to pep one up, only stick in an antibiotic when there is a virus. Today I have to go to the dentist, the first of four who has consented to take me on after four weeks of trying on my part, and shall hear what he has decided to do from brooding over the x-rays. I suspect I have reached the stage where I shall have to wear the rabbit-trap, and that may be a relief after all the breaking of attachments and crumbling of single teeth at important moments. I shall simply have a spare set to bring out in a crisis.

A few weeks ago the Eynsham Scoundrel came to light again. I found a letter from him stuck in the door inviting us to dinner at the house where he was staying in a plushy suburb on the other side of the Harbour. I didn't reply. Did you find out any more about his mysterious activities? Have also had a letter and a book of poems from Louis Johnson. I expect they will want to descend too. Please don't send any more as it happens at the rate of several a week. All very well in the 19th Century if one had a chain-gang of minions. Somebody has threatened us with Isaiah Berlin, but I hope he will be too taken up with the universities.

Believe it or not I have been invited as a kind of professor to Berkeley Calif! Strangers get the oddest idea of what one is like.

One visit I enjoyed was from Professor F. Page, who got in touch while he in Sydney for some concerts. I'm sorry it was so brief as I like him very much but

SELLING FOOD & COOKERY

TO MARKET, TO MARKET

In the days when food was fuel and was either available or not, selling it required no great skill. Settlers brought their produce to market and hoped for a good price; or sold it by some more convenient means. Marketing was always subject to the mood of the times, as an advertisement from the *Sydney Gazette* of 20 April 1806 shows. (This was just after disastrous floods on the Hawkesbury River had left the young colony once again hungry.)

WHEAT.

Richard Palmer, Brickfield Hill, gives notice to families in immediate want of a small supply of wheat, that he is in possession of about 30 bushels, which he is desirous of distributing in suitable proportions at the prices fixed by His Excellency's General Order, and he at the same time assures the public that any further supplies he may receive during the existence of scarcity shall be distributed in like manner.

In these times the arrival in port of a ship bringing supplies of flour, tea and other basics was an event of real importance. 'Shipping intelligence' and notices of ships' cargoes for sale to the public were eagerly sought. Mere announcement was enough. Retailers sold from stalls or shops, or hawked their goods in the streets. Always the public was assured of quality that was superior, the finest or 'not to be surpassed in the colony'—and of prices that were the 'lowest possible', or never more than 'moderate'. Energetic traders sometimes resorted to various advertising gimmicks, like the following rather flamboyant one from the *Sydney Morning Herald* of 3 April 1850.

This 1960s promotional booklet boasted '107 exciting, nutritious recipes'
(Sydney: New South Wales Milk Board, 1963)

(above left) By the 1880s shipping and distribution links were bringing an ever-increasing variety of products to Australian tables
Queen's Wharf, Melbourne c.1888
Phillip-Stephan Photo-Lith. and Typographic Process Company
coloured photolithograph; 28.8 x 36.5 cm
From the Pictorial Collection

RECALLING THE FRUIT & VEG WAR

Sometimes the local providoring competition could get hot, as evidenced by James Castrission's recollection of his Greek cafe and fruit-and-veg shop business in Gundagai, NSW, in the decades straddling the Second World War.

... We heard someone was coming to open up [a fruit and veg shop in] opposition to us. Next door ... he was going to open a shop against the Castrission brothers, 'and I'm going to break them', he said. We heard this and of course I didn't like it but still, I said, alright, let them come ... we were lucky that we met an Italian fellow, Venzella from Batlow. We used to buy potatoes from him before he went away, and that particular time he said to me 'I'm going to Coffs Harbour'. 'Well,' I said, 'Coffs Harbour. You'll be able to help us from over there...' He [sent] us bananas, tomatoes, pineapples from there. Beautiful stuff. Bananas were four and six a case ...

Anyway, the fruit war started ... this was really a war that reduced ten years of my life ... I was lucky to get Venzella to help me for this war. Direct from the grower, tomatoes. And he used to sell beautiful tomatoes for tenpence per pound before Christmas ... beautiful stuff. Look I was selling them and I was saying 'Oh what a shame selling them tenpence.' They were one and threepence in Sydney ... And ... [the other seller] had all the rubbish in the world coming down here ... And oranges, he started 50 for a shilling. We did the same. Customers used to go and say we want 50 oranges for a shilling. 'I'm sorry, we're right out.' Tricks like that, you see. Until they used to come to us and we used to give it to them. ... good seven bananas about that big, for a shilling. You only needed three customers to sell one big case. Look, the amount of stuff that we sold during that fruit war, it was tremendous. All the downstairs was as big as the shop, it was full of stuff, mostly fruit. We used to get tomatoes, truckloads, bananas the same ...

... And also we had a good show in the window. Fruit business is one of the hardest that you can get any day... it's all hard work. And anyway, in six weeks I finished him off and he had to close down, but I kept up the prices quite reasonable. I had from Albury people coming to buy fruit in my place and it was in ... the Sun—about it: 'If you want any cheap bananas, go to Gundagai and get them.' [Laughs.]

PROCLAMATION.
GOD SAVE THE QUEEN.

I, EDWIN CAMPBELL, by this advertisement do inform the inhabitants of Sydney and the vicinity, that after great labour and expense I have succeeded in finishing an apparatus for roasting coffee; and having obtained the opinion of several scientific gentlemen, feel justified in asserting that it is the best method ever introduced.

... The price of the coffee, after being roasted in this manner, is only 8d. per lb., and warranted the best in Sydney. For the greater convenience of purchasers I have taken the premises No. 487, George-street, eight doors from Hunter-street, lately occupied by Mr Milatovich, tailor. The establishment will open for the sale of the coffee, also tea, sugars, spices, and other groceries of the best quality, at moderate prices, on Saturday next, April 6, 1850. Those who relish a good cup of coffee are encouraged to purchase just one pound as a test.

Observe! opposite the Barrack Gate, No. 487.

N.B.—Not connected with any other house in George-street.

By the end of the nineteenth century, many food advertisements were using graphics to attract attention, and were appealing to what were perceived to be the particular needs or concerns of consumers. Assurances of quality were extended to include purity. (Although claims were often exaggerated, there was good reason to emphasise quality and purity: hygiene, especially in the meat and dairy industries, and adulteration of food, were matters of rising public concern until effective controls were introduced from the early 1900s.)

Christmas and Easter in particular were opportunities not to be missed by advertisers, as indicated by the *Sydney Morning Herald* of 7 April 1909. (Note that, as far as imported seafood was concerned, 'fresh' meant tinned; otherwise it was salted or smoked. The word is still often used somewhat imaginatively by foodsellers.)

Fish for Good Friday
You'll want fish on Friday next. Make certain of the punctual delivery of your requirements ...
Fresh 'spring' salmon from Canada
English kippers and bloaters
English soles
N.Z. blue cod (Fresh or Smoked)
N.Z. barracouta ...

In the twentieth century we have seen a parade of promotional campaigns sponsored by various government-industry marketing boards or industry associations. Many of these have been designed to persuade Australians to increase their consumption of particular foods. One approach has been the use of competitions, designed both to boost sales and to gather market intelligence, as in the following instance from the *South Australian Advertiser* of 16 October 1918:

DRIED FRUITS
... WANTED—A NAME
A Big Contest ...
The Australian Dried Fruits Association (A.D.F.A.) realises that the Australian Public (through lack of information) regards Dried Fruit (especially Sultanas, Currants, and Lexias) as a Luxury instead of a Necessity—a Food.
The A.D.F.A. is undertaking a big Publicity Campaign to bring their Raisins (S., C. & L.) under the direct notice of adults and children.
One of the first steps is to ADOPT A BRAND OR A NAME, by which the fruit will be known from one end of Australia to the other.
In California there is the 'Sun-Maid Raisin' and the 'Sunkist Orange.'
Some such striking and appropriate name is wanted for the Superior Australian Sun-Dried Products
—Attractive—Appetising—Clean—Luscious—Nourishing—Satisfying—produced in the Irrigation Districts of the Commonwealth.
[Competition for name; prizes P25, P10, and lesser amounts. Must send 3/- for which a 3/- pack of all three fruits will be sent; or buy from grocer and send proof with entry.]
Competitors will therefore be able to judge the merits of the fruits they are helping to popularise; and will provide a fine Xmas treat for themselves.
Entries must reach Mildura by 30th November, 1918 ...

CREATING DEMAND

At the time of settlement, the sale of prepared food was already an old tradition in Europe—and it took almost no time to appear here. On 25 November 1804, the *Sydney Gazette* published the following 'notice':

The inhabitants of the Town of Sydney are respectfully informed, that excellent and well-constructed Mutton Pyes are ready for issue at the shop of William Chapman, High Street, every day at twelve precisely; the superior excellence of which will, it is hoped, maintain a decided preference. Newmade Sausages, &c. constantly supplied.

This is not to suggest that Australia was always a fast-food paradise. The reality was more low-key, as suggested by the following, from the *Sydney Morning Herald* of 15 August 1831:

Notice.—The Public are respectfully informed, that Cooper's Steam Engine will open for Grinding and Dressing Wheat in any quantities, from the First of August next, from which date there will be constantly on Sale, First and Second Flour, of the best quality, Pollard and Bran, at reduced prices ...

(The notice, incidentally, was followed immediately by a request for a miller, 'who thoroughly understands his Business, and can write a plain hand'.)

Australian food processing began with basics like milling flour, salting meat and making cheese, then moved on to canning meat, jam and fruit for export. By the early twentieth century, ingredients such as cornflour, baking powder and breakfast cereal were being heavily promoted, soon followed by an ever-expanding range of convenience foods. Mere announcement of the product's availability was no longer sufficient, nor was the simple repetition of slogans in the top and bottom margins of cookery books. In an increasingly competitive and sophisticated market, advertising strategies were becoming more calculated. The goal of marketing was not simply to sell what was available—but to create *demand*. The impact on cooking and eating patterns was to be profound.

Australia's Golden Circle company was one which took a lead in promoting their product this way. (See feature opposite.) The rice-growing industry similarly promoted its product: about the same time that Australians were learning to put pineapple pieces into their sweet-and-sour pork, they were also being taught to cook 'fluffy', rather than 'gluggy' rice to go with it. (In fact, if cooks of the time had followed with no more than reasonable care the methods their grandmothers had used for cooking rice, they would have found that the 'fluffiness' and 'glugginess' actually have more to do with the variety of rice than with cooking method.) In the interests of eating more Australian rice, however, they were now persuaded to boil it in copious quantities of water, then pour much of its nutrient down the sink. But as a marketing strategy, it worked: we all ate more rice.

(*above*) This 1920s advertisement shows a more extended use of the commercial illustrator's art
From *Dainty Dishes* promotional recipe booklet

(*below*) Sheet music for a song extolling the breakfast cereal Weet-Bix
From the Music Collection

PUSHING THE PINEAPPLE

In his book *One Continuous Picnic: A History of Eating in Australia* (1982), Michael Symons described how the young Golden Circle company, facing bleak prospects for the export of processed pineapple in the 1950s, set about expanding its home market in a well-planned and sustained campaign to change Australians' food habits. The product range—principally rings (the 'golden circles', of course), segments and crush in cans, juice in bottles and cans, and later 'tropical fruit salad' in cans—was designed to reduce waste and increase the company's exposure on the shelves of self-service food stores.

The market strategy combined three tactics which have since become favourites in the food industry. First, the advertisers tried to dissociate pineapple from other canned fruits—so as to avoid direct competition and a possible price war. Second, a program of regular sales promotions aimed to boost demand when stocks were high (just after processing) or needed to be cleared (just before harvest). Third, consumers were encouraged to extend their use of pineapple, helped along by plenty of recipes. The consumers themselves supplied many of these: in 1958, for instance, *The Australian Women's Weekly* ran a cookery competition for recipes containing pineapple. In its issue of 10 September of that year, the prize-winning recipes were published alongside an advertisement proclaiming 'Big *Women's Weekly* recipe competition proved most cooks use Golden Circle pineapple'.

This booklet from the 1950s *(right)* formed part of Golden Circle's extensive promotional campaign—the company seen working here in unison with the manufacturers of Carnation Milk to persuade Australians to concoct a pineapple pavlova

(below) Another instance of a manufacturer promoting extended use of their product was the Campbell company's book *Treasury of Recipes: 500 Wonderful 'Cooking with Soup' Recipes* which included, among many suggestions, cakes made with tomato soup (Sydney: Southern Cross International, 195–)

The strategy was a huge success. Many Australians will remember the days when grilled pineapple rings routinely appeared with sausages for breakfast; pineapple was found in sandwiches or salads at lunch, in cake fillings at afternoon tea, in sweet-and-sour pork for dinner and, of course, in all manner of sweets. Other favourites of the time were pineapple pies, pineapple jam, and ham-and-pineapple pizza.

The success of the Golden Circle campaign can be seen quite clearly reflected in the Presbyterian cookery book of New South Wales. In 1950, 16 of its recipes called for pineapple. In 1979 most of them were still there, though more than 130 other non-pineapple recipes had been dropped for lack of interest. Ten new pineapple recipes had been added, nearly all for meat or vegetable dishes. (The same book, incidentally, also shows how Australians had earlier been persuaded to extend their use of bananas: in 1939 there were just three recipes for banana; all sweets. By 1950 there were 18, including cakes, jam, curry, chicken Maryland and pickles.)

CONVENIENCE FOOD

Ever since William Chapman had advertised his 'well-constructed Mutton Pyes' back in 1804, urban Australians have never been far from supplies of ready-to-eat food of one sort or another. The most famous was the ordinary meat pie, which reigned supreme in the mid–twentieth century and was regarded by many as our national dish. (See feature, p. 68.) Perhaps the most infamous of the fast foods was the Chiko roll—a distant, and very Australian, adaptation of the Asian spring roll, which could be bought deep-fried from fish-and-chip and hamburger shops. In the 1970s these 'native' foods were challenged

by American fast-food chains selling fried chicken, pizza and hamburgers—sweeping into Australia and quickly establishing long-term dominance of the industry. Alternatives such as Lebanese flat breads with meat or vegetarian fillings have also established their own strong following.

Convenience is served in more forms than takeaway food. Most of the early kitchen innovations were concerned with ingredients and process. Baking powder replaced bicarbonate of soda and acid, and was followed a few decades later by self-raising flour. Starch-based custard powder (coloured yellow) took over from real egg custard. Prepared gelatine did away with the tedium of boiling calves' feet to make jelly. Temperature-controlled ovens reduced the guess-work of baking, and such devices as mixing machines made kitchen life easier.

Although bottled sauces and pickles were on sale at least as early as the 1830s, their purchase was long considered a luxury; most households made their own. Recipes for tomato sauce, pickles and chutneys abounded well into the twentieth century—though gradually here too the manufacturers won, and today we can select from an astonishing array on the supermarket shelves. The same story can be told of jams and confectionery.

And much the same happened to the main course of meat and vegetables: gradually the work was taken over by industry. Pork or veal or turkey for roasting was sold already rolled and stuffed with dried fruit; beef for 'goulash' was provided in already cut strips; lamb and chicken cubes pre-skewered and smothered in bottled marinades. The choice of meat dish came to be controlled less by the cook's imagination or cookery book, and more by what the butcher had prepared and put in the window. Vegetables too came 'freshly frozen' and ready to cook—provoking vigorous retaliation by the greengrocers and, in turn, yet further innovations from the food companies.

The push continues: pasta sauces of all kinds can be bought ready-made, 'fresh' pasta comes sealed in plastic and will keep in the refrigerator for weeks until wanted, and frozen pizzas can be finished in the microwave in minutes ...

(from top)
'Don't they ever stop eating for an hour or two? ... They eat walking about, eat in bed, eat while they work.'
Donald Friend (1914–89)
From 'Ayam-Ayam Kesayangan' (Donald Friend Diaries)
From the Manuscript Collection

Cappuccinos, pizzas, hamburgers and souvlaki, all at one stall in Queen Victoria Markets, Melbourne
Photograph by Francis Reiss
From the Pictorial Collection

Fast food heaven: Kentucky Fried Chicken and Uniting Church, Cowra
Photograph by Brendon Kelson
Regional Cities and Major Towns Project
From the Pictorial Collection

Gladys Timbs (b.1905) and husband established 'The Gum Leaf' cake shops in New South Wales: in the Manly Corso from 1932, with later ones in Chatswood and Maitland. Below, she recalls selling meat pies—and on the page opposite she talks about making cakes.

... everybody's got their own recipe for pies and their own recipe for the pastry that goes on them ... we made the genuine Sargeant's pies ... It was between a flake and a short [pastry]. It was a special pie crust ... it wasn't sweet, it wasn't short, and it wasn't flaky, it was just a crust that would hold the pie together and not break up as you ate it, let the gravy all run down the front of you—and then each pie had to have so much [meat] in it, so many ounces in it ...

Inspectors would come in and open up a pie and see what was in it, and send it away to be analysed—oh goodness there's a lot of rules and regulations in opening a pie shop ... It's not just easy going ... They weren't as particular about [sausage rolls and pasties] as they were with meat pies, but we never ever got into any trouble.

We used to make sandwiches in the summertime when the pies dropped off, and then in the winter time you'd sell six times more pies than you would a sandwich ... Only have to rain and you'd sell meat pies, doesn't matter if it's hot or cold, if it's raining, you'd sell meat pies.

I remember [my husband] Stan going to Canberra [during the Second World War] to try and get the tax off meat pies—which we eventually did—meat pies, sausage rolls and pasties, the tax came off that ... we paid tax on cakes because that was luxury ... but see, pies and that—well, was a natural thing wasn't it: Australian pie for lunch. [They were considered an] essential ...

Counter-lunch at the Fitzroy Hotel, Melbourne, featuring the meat pie in formal mode (requiring use of cutlery)
Australian Information Service
From the Pictorial Collection

MEAT PIE: AN AUSTRALIAN 'ESSENTIAL'

As versatile as the sandwich, the meat pie could be eaten with one hand—the epicure struggling to keep the filling within the pastry while walking down the street or cheering on at a football match. Alternatively the pie could be ordered with chips and peas in a café, and eaten in style with knife and fork. Mini-pies arrived later, bought frozen and reheated to serve as party snacks. Although the meat pie was traditionally improved with a dollop of bottled tomato sauce, other garnishes have at times also been suggested. A visiting *cordon bleu* expert in the 1970s suggested that it might be turned into something approaching a dainty dish by placing a layer of cooked red cabbage on top of the meat filling just before serving. In Adelaide, the pie featured in the nearest Australia has probably come to having an authentic regional specialty—the *floater*. (Though some might say only because nowhere else on earth has anyone seen the merit of serving a meat pie *in* pea soup, rather than *after* it.)

HAVING YOUR CAKE

Another area revolutionised by convenience has been cake-making. If the numbers of recipes in successive editions of the New South Wales Presbyterian cookery book can be taken as a guide, home cake-making was at its most popular in the two decades between the wars. It is perhaps ironic that the art of cake-making reached its peak just before the revolution of kitchen technology began to take the hard work and uncertainty out of it. By the time mixing appliances and temperature-controlled ovens became common, cooks had already turned their attention elsewhere. Small cakes and biscuits were more convenient to make (and to ration to children): their popularity rose as that of large cakes sank. Those who still wanted the large ones were able to save time and effort by using packaged cake mixes, encouraged by heavy advertising and cookery competitions. (One such event celebrating the cookery skills of Australian housewives was the Butter–White Wings Bake-Off competition, run a number of times during the 1960s. A cake of the time—the *peach kuchen*—was a good example of a product's 'extended use': it had a butter-cake mix in the base, and tinned peaches in the topping.)

Packaged pastry mixes also appeared, then frozen pastry. But by the 1970s there seemed little need to bake at home at all. Shops selling cakes and pastry had been around longer than anyone remembered—now they were joined by frozen cakes and pastries in the supermarkets to offer the ultimate in convenience.

(left) The joy of cake-making
Harold Cazneaux (1878–1953)
Patricia Minchin Holding Cake
Cazneaux Collection; from the Pictorial Collection

A CAKE SHOP IN THE CORSO

Many readers will recognise Gladys Timbs' 'Viennese tarts' (described below) as the familiar Neenish (or Neinish or Nienich) tarts which seem to be peculiarly Australian, but whose precise origin is still debated from time to time. The tarts are still found in many shops, but as Mrs Timbs explains, they were fiddly things to make. The really distinctive thing about them was not their half-white, half-brown icing—that was a familiar decoration for cakes and biscuits long before Neenish tarts appeared. Rather, it was their almond pastry and the idea of a soft cream filling underneath the icing.

... we had a good everyday trade, and then Sunday and holidays of course you could hardly keep up with it. You had to work day and night to make enough stock to last you, and then if you struck a wet weekend you'd have all that stuff and what would you do— go to the piggery, because [there was] no refrigeration then to keep it ... there was ... very little pure cream, and you could only [make up the cream] when the customer came in ... because the cream would go sour.

... we sold small cakes for one and six a dozen ... small cakes were always very popular ... Cup cakes ... were the cheapest cake, ninepence a dozen, and then one and six were fancy cakes, and we made apple pies and custard tarts and all those sort of things, a huge variety.

... every night before I left the shop I used to make two trays of Viennese tarts, and they were the fiddling things, they'd never pay you to employ anybody to make them because you made them with a special pastry ... you rolled them out and you cut them up, put them on to the tray, baked it, take it out—that's twice you've handled it—take it out of the pan, put it on a wire—and it's three times you've handled it—cream it—that's four times—pick it up again and do one half white, pick it up again and do one half chocolate ... that's six times you handled a little cake like that, and got a penny halfpenny for it!

SWEET FRUIT SPICED SCONES

❦

Sift 4 level cups self-raising flour, 1 teaspoon salt and 1 teaspoon mixed spices, add 6 tablespoons sugar, rub in 2 tablespoons butter, beat 1 egg well, add 1 1/4 cups milk to beaten egg, add 1/2 cup sultanas and 1/2 cup currants to flour. Pour beaten egg and milk gently into prepared flour and mix lightly with a knife, turn out and knead just a little to make a smooth dough. With hands, press the dough out lightly 3/4 in. thick, cut out with round or square cutter. Allow scones to stand 8 mins., bake 15 to 20 mins. in fairly quick oven. When cooked, glaze on top with a little butter and allow scones to remain on tray until cold.

—Secret of Success Cookery Book

The above work, published in recent years, collected Mrs Floate's celebrated recipes from the 1930s and 1940s (Victoria: Greenhouse Publications, 1985)

(bottom) A tea party in 1940s country Victoria, around the time of Mrs Floate's ascendancy
Photograph by Australian Information Service
Drouin Town and Rural Life during World War Two
From the Pictorial Collection

THE UNSINKABLE MRS FLOATE

Australia's champion cake-maker was arguably Mrs Dorothy Floate of Benalla in Victoria, who practised her art over many decades, and repeatedly proved it in cookery competitions such as those in country agricultural shows.

In 1939 she won a prize of £100 for her rainbow block cake, in the *Women's Weekly* recipe competition. Mrs Floate was the wife of a guard in the Victorian railways, and in her travels around Victoria had learned to cook under primitive conditions, as revealed in an interview made at the time:

> 'When I was married first at Beaufort I had only a camp oven,' she said. 'This is a vessel with three legs which you hung up the chimney over an open fire and then pile hot coals on the top of it.
>
> 'But all the same one of the best ducks I ever turned out came out of a camp oven.
>
> 'I was very sorry when I decided that I had no further use for the oven, and I gave it away to a tramp. It was like parting with an old friend.'
>
> Mrs. Floate then used a colonial oven which has a fire on top all the time, but for baking a fire must be put underneath as well.
>
> She cooked then on various wood stoves, trying new recipes all the time, and it was only seven years ago that she began using up-to-date stoves.
>
> *—The Australian Women's Weekly,* 27 May 1939

While she was being interviewed, Mrs Floate was also cooking the family dinner: roast lamb, baked potatoes, cabbage, green peas and beans, followed by a rice custard for pudding. Her cooking skills were not confined to cakes—in the 1930s and 1940s she published a series of modestly produced little *Secret of Success* cookery books. (Later collected and reissued in a work published in 1985.) By the time the first volume went to press, she was able to claim having taken 1284 prizes.

DINING OUT: THE EATING EXPERIENCE

On 18 July 1850 a promotion in the *Sydney Morning Herald* announced:

> A splendid Baron of Beef and Plum Pudding will be on the table at One o'clock, This Day,
> at Entwhistle's Hotel.

The advertisement is indicative that by the mid–nineteenth century colonial eating establishments were learning to 'extend' their range of uses. Hungry travellers could be joined at such hostelries by local monied folk who appreciated superior food and the convenience of dining in the city. As a further indication, ten years later a luncheon in the café at Tattersall's Hotel offered the following bill of fare:

> Roast duck and green peas Roast and boiled fowls
> Roast lamb Ditto veal Ditto beef Boiled mutton
> Corn beef Ox tongues York hams

Tattersall's served 'teas and suppers' till 11 pm; chops, steaks, and kidneys could be procured at all hours during the day, and a 'first class ordinary' was available in the long room at 1 pm daily. By the turn of the century the same establishment was offering the following 'Dinner in Town':

> Oysters on shell Soup Fish Entree Joints Poultry
> Sweets Cheese and Salad Fruits of season
> Muscatels and Almonds

Similar stories were being told in all the Australian cities, and over the next 100 years cafés, hotel dining rooms, restaurants and other eating places were gradually extended in two directions. First, in the range and type of food they served. While some clients simply wanted to eat, others could be attracted by a *table d'hôte* offering plain but satisfying fare that may no longer have been practical in the domestic economy of a small household. (Entwhistle's baron of beef and plum pudding, for example). Many again were, and still are,

(above) The obvious attraction of ethnic restaurants was getting food you couldn't cook at home, as here at Sydney's Japanese restaurant, Suehiro, in the 1970s
Photograph by John Tanner;
Australian Information Service
From the Pictorial Collection

(left) Interior of a dining saloon. Most major city emporiums also had tea houses and cafés
Brady Collection; from the Pictorial Collection

(above) Tourist resorts offered fine wining and dining
in special surrounds
Charles Henry Hunt (1857–1938)
Advertising poster 1920s
coloured photomechanical print; 70 x 95.5 cm
From the Pictorial Collection

(right) An elegantly scripted 1920s menu which,
despite hand-drawn, coloured kookaburra motif,
reveals a decidedly French leaning
From the Ephemera Collection

lured by a promise of something different—food they wouldn't, or couldn't, cook at home (today one of the special attractions of the 'ethnic' restaurants). And, of course, there are also those who can be enticed by a search for excellence and the chance to become gourmets for a night.

The second direction of extension has been in the range of occasions on which people might eat out. The 'occasion' has increasingly become a potent marketing tool, as restaurants have found that their best business has not simply been selling food to hungry people, but selling the *eating experience*, in all its variety. 'Food-as-fuel' gives way to hospitality.

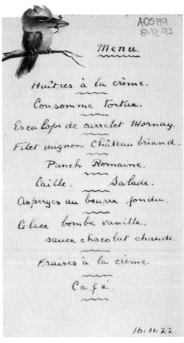

SOMETHING SWEET

As Gay Bilson comments (at right), desserts are often the afterthought—the 'glamour' side of cookery being the main course. Though desserts and puddings have always had strong representation in the cookery books, and some recent stylishly presented texts have focused solely on preparation of attractively presented and tasty sweets.

At home, too, old favourites such as sago or bread-and-butter pudding can occasionally hold out against frozen cheesecakes or plastic buckets of icecream. And even older classics can be recycled, as in 1993, when prize-winning apprentice chef Simon Le Comte served up a raspberry and Brie brioche on glaze savayon inspired by a recipe which he had found in an eighteenth-century French recipe book in the National Library's collection.

DESSERTS

... I have a theory that we should get the sweet thing over with at the beginning of the meal—that sugar drowns other flavours. For instance ... you might have a small glass of Barsac or a fruity sweet wine to start a meal—as you would have a dry sherry, for instance, or a glass of champagne. So that's your sugar over and done with—and then you could get on with the serious things, which are savoury.

... It's a difficult area ... being a dessert chef is seen as rather the lowest of the low, really, in a kitchen—there aren't many kids out there who say: 'I'm interested in making pastry and doing desserts. Could I do that?'—everyone wants to do main courses and be the star. —Gay Bilson

(clockwise from immediate left)
ACT apprentice chef Simon Le Comte won a medal for his raspberry and Brie brioche on glaze savayon. Photograph by Martin Jones (detail)

Christine Manfield's *Paramount Desserts* does desserts with pizazz
(Ringwood: Penguin, 1997)

Neapolitan ices, grape sorbets and Nesselrode pudding, from *The Australasian Cookery Book*
(Melbourne: Ward, Lock & Co, 1913).

'Grand dinner style' sweets from *Mrs Beeton's All-About Cookery*
(Melbourne: Ward, Lock & Co, 1923)

BREAD-AND-BUTTER PUDDING, BAKED

The humble makings of a one-time household favourite.

Cut off the crust of 5 or 6 thin slices of bread and butter and divide each slice of bread into 4 squares, arrange them in layers in a well-buttered pie-dish, and sprinkle each layer with sultanas or whatever dried fruit is being used. Beat 2 eggs, add 1 dessert-spoonful of sugar, stir until dissolved, then mix in 1 pint of milk and pour gently over the bread, which should only half fill the dish. Let it stand at least 1 hour for the bread to soak, then bake in a moderately cool oven for nearly 1 hour.

—*The Australasian Cookery Book*, 1913

THE ART OF THE RESTAURATEUR: BEROWRA WATERS INN

Gay Bilson

Gay Bilson reflects on the experience of running the Berowra Waters Inn on a tributary of the Hawkesbury river north of Sydney, from the 1970s. The building was modified by architect Glenn Murcutt, and the ambience of the restaurant, accessed by car, boat and flying boat, was a key element of the act of dining there.

Berowra Waters Inn restaurant opened in March 1977 and closed 18 years later in March 1995. Tony Bilson and I had sold the Bon Goût in Sydney (1973–76) and gone to the river in January 1977. Tony Bilson was chef until 1981. When he left I bought out his share and, following a short period when Andrew Birley did the main courses, Janni Kyritsis held the position of chef until the restaurant's last day.

In its early years I cooked too (first courses and desserts), and ran the restaurant. But, as cooks better than myself began to work there—Leigh Stone Herbert, for example—I got out of the kitchen except for desserts, and went into the dining room, while also retaining control of the menu. By the late 1980s I was only cooking when I had to, but still did the menu with Kyritsis. It was in this period that I began to see myself as a restaurateur rather than a cook, and these same years saw the 'flowering' of Janni Kyritsis. His role in the restaurant should not be underestimated: he maintained standards of cooking, inspired the young cooks who came to work there and set an extraordinary example of never-flagging work. It just happened to be my restaurant.

In retrospect, my role, in caring so passionately about the restaurant's parts (architecture, menu, service, staff) and keeping it viable, was to ask the people

... We're going to die anyway—let's just simply use our lives as fully as possible, hopefully as humanely as possible ... Restaurants don't matter, which is why I'm quoted as saying: 'For God's sake, it's only a restaurant', when I put [Berowra Waters Inn] up for sale and it caused such a lot of fuss— but as long as they're there and people need to eat, and they do, then we should try and do it as well as possible, and with great passion

(left) Gay Bilson at the river in 1987
Photograph by Sally Hassan

(opposite page) Set against a gum-stacked hill and accessible only by water, Berowra Waters Inn was designed in 'Australian vernacular', featuring a corrugated iron roof and a verandah, and utilising bolted metal and sandstone materials
Photograph by Grant Mudford

who worked there to give as passionately as myself. Because the building was in such a difficult and different environment, everyone who worked there took on family-like roles. When we were slow in the winter, for instance, the waiters might clear the gutters or clean the roof. The cooks might turn over the work boat and scrub it, or clear away the bush from the back of the building. We fought bush fires together. In the last six years Murray Smith, the manager and *sommelier*, set the same kind of example as Kyritsis. They were both great problem-solvers, and are wonderful people.

Berowra Waters Inn was particular to its time: the early years of what has now become a lively and confident restaurant scene in Australian cities. People like myself were, in a sense, the mothers and fathers of it all. In this role we sent young cooks out into the world and a new generation began to drive the food industry in Sydney from the late 1980s.

I do see that the parochial history books want to remember the Inn for great dishes, its dedicated kitchen and so on, and in part they are right. But that's not the way I remember it at all. It was years of physically hard work and a sense of separation from the city: unconnected, dedicated. It was dominated by the weather, the water, the building, the boats, solving the problems of septic and kitchen waste. Also continuous years of building and of a joyful relationship with Glenn Murcutt, the architect. Berowra Waters Inn made no one rich! When I sold it I was still paying off the last loan—but then all that ever mattered was that there should be enough money to keep it going.

People who came to eat there remember it with the same kind of affection I felt for it. I think this is because we, the workers, understood that the effort our diner had to make in order to arrive at the restaurant, the price they needed to pay for their meal, should be respected. We felt the need to thank them for coming. We all gave, including the diners.

I'm not the best person to sum up Berowra Waters Inn, but neither are the journalists. I knew to stay there for years and years, and I knew to end it.

Perhaps I'm a very savvy myth-maker.

ON ROMANTIC PROVIDORING

When I first went [to Berowra Waters] I romantically thought that, being close to a market gardening area ... I would be able to simply knock on people's door and have perfect fruits and vegetables—having listened to various stories from ex-French waiters, one in particular who came from the Beaujolais area and used to have to go out and pick the beans when they were no longer than his little finger [but the best produce went off to the markets and I didn't pursue any relationships between growers and the kitchen. Too much on my plate on the river.] ... A long time ago, local fishermen would fish for bream and blackfish and still-live tiny prawns. That didn't work out particularly, either. [Though] it was terrific at its time, and romantic for diners to see them arrive with a large old cane washing basket full of fish that are so much more fresh than [the] markets, and the prawns still jumping out of the basket ...

ON 'STRANGE MEATS'

I think I'm always going to be remembered for strange meats [such as stuffed pig's ears]. [The chef] Janni and I were both saying, 'This is absolutely delicious. Give it a go'. Also Janni very much likes doing things which are almost wrapped or packaged ... the work that goes on in the kitchen ... is to do with craft. So, if we served a pig's trotter, Janni would bone it; if we did a braised and then deep-fried quail, we'd bone the quail and decide how much was needed, make some sort of paste to bind the meats together, and roll it again. A lot of trouble is gone to in the kitchen ...

ON AMBIENCE

I certainly don't view myself primarily as a cook, which is why I asked you to describe me as a restaurateur. I'm interested in all the details of the table, and the table in the dining room, and the dining room's place in its environment ... My contribution, I like to think, is one of good taste—in the serious definition of that term, not its lesser and trivial definition ... it's like setting the stage ... but you're also setting the auditorium, the theatre ... What I hope we've done at Berowra Waters is introduce a reverence for the cliff and the water and the architecture of the dining room, on to the same level as that of the food, without actually pointing it out to anyone—so that, romantically, you could still be surprised by it all ...

I have very strong ideas about the way the food is served, how we treat the diner, across all levels of ... the restaurant, including the whole aesthetic of the dining room and sense of welcome and leave-taking, and all that sort of thing. It doesn't suit everyone, but I won't compromise ... We've never worked like that, so in that sense we're part of a small group of people who please the few—but those few are enough. I mean, Australia has an extraordinarily small population, and I'm incredibly grateful that there are enough people to enjoy eating [at Berowra Waters] ... that we have enough support to keep on going

WHAT'S COOKING NOW

CONTEMPORARY CULTURE

If you could line up on a single shelf all the cookery books published in Australia's short literary history, what would you notice? First, of course, it would have to be a very long shelf.

You might then notice that just a few centimetres of shelf space would be quite enough to hold all the books produced in the first 100 years of settlement. And the next 50 years would probably take up no more space than the last 50 weeks. What was once a trickle of cookery books has more recently become a torrent. What are people *doing* with them? Anything but cook, it seems. It has been commented that few people who buy a new cookery book nowadays ever make more than a couple of dishes from it—often not even that.

THE ART OF THE COOKERY BOOK: TRANSFORMATIONS

Another thing you would notice as you ran your eye along the shelf would be a dramatic change in the *look* of the books. The early ones were generally small, cheaply produced works (often with advertisements to help meet printing costs), crammed with text and devoid of illustrations. Seriously dull. In the modern market there is still a place for serious and plain books—but the ones which seem to sell best are large, stylish, attractively laid out and lavishly colour-illustrated works. Those which reach out and grab you from the shelf. The art of cookery has inspired the art of the cookery book. Though, indeed, art and food have often consorted together.

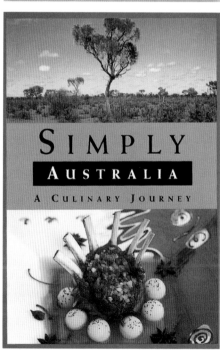

You would also find many other changes. Early on your way along the shelf, you would find works such as the Presbyterian Women's Missionary Association's *Cookery Book of Good and Tried Receipts* (1896), with an eye to the strictness of domestic economy and the rectitude of its golden rules. Featuring plain practicality:

> When breaking eggs, it is advisable to break them one at a time into a saucer, emptying each one from the saucer as soon as you ascertain that it is quite fresh. By this means you avoid the annoying accident of having one egg that is not quite fresh spoil half a dozen that are.

As well as plain economy:

> A pinch of carbonate of soda added when stewing fruit saves sugar.

(It neutralises some of the natural acids so that the fruit tastes less tart.)

Further along the cookbook shelf, there would be other kinds of practicality: cooking for two, cooking for hordes, cooking on a tight budget, cooking in a hurry ...

Some recent samples of the art of the cookery book. The repackaging of the recipes of an earlier generation in *Recipes My Mother Gave Me*, Stephanie Alexander's reissue of Mary Burchett's cookery book (Ringwood: Penguin Books Australia, 1997), and Michael Ryan's 'exploratory' approach in *Simply Australia: A Culinary Journey* (New Holland Publishers/C.J. Publishing, 1997)

You would also encounter some of the exactitude of science—including cookery by numbers—and a daunting display of advice on diet and nutrition.

You would find most ethnic cuisines represented in the shelf's later years. Many books would mark the gradual discovery of the food and cookery of the Middle East and Asia—first with crude approximations of ingredient and method, then with earnest searches for authenticity, and finally with the convenient adaptations of industry and popular taste. (We may pause to wonder whether future food writers will compare Australia's 'Thai curry' to its 'Indian curry' of recent—and unlamented—memory.)

In short, the bookshelf would tell the story of the transformation of food and cookery—from an English imposition, to an Australian way of life—from provision of fuel, to popular culture.

FOOD FOR PLEASURE

We have already seen that the English ideal began to give way to the Australian reality somewhere about the time of Federation. The point at which the serious business of kitchen work began—slowly but surely—to give way to the *joy* of food is also not hard to find. Give or take a year or two, it was 1952.

By then the Second World War was seven years past, the task of 'post-war reconstruction' was well under way, the price of wool was headed towards the magical 'pound per pound', and Australia was rejoicing in an unprecedented baby boom. There were steady jobs for all, and Australians looked to the future with quiet confidence. New appliances were reducing the drudgery of cooking, cleaning, washing and ironing; refrigerators were a luxury nearly everyone could now afford.

It was around this time that a cheeky little book titled *Oh, For a French Wife!* made its appearance, and quickly blew away any mystique surrounding 'Continental' cookery. Its creators—Ted Moloney, Deke Coleman and George Molnar (who provided the drawings)—tried to make cookery *fun*. The trio explained how to eat artichokes. ('Not for one moment,' they warned, 'do we mean those knobbly little runts of things that look something like potatoes, taste like crushed ants and are sometimes known as Jerusalem artichokes.' Though even those knobbly little runts have today found a place in our post-modernist cookery.) The trio also introduced the matter of wine in cooking, this way:

> In Brussels there's a famous statue of a little boy. It's really a fountain. You know, the one that's widely reproduced on postcards with the advice, 'Never drink water'. That advice needs rounding off with five more words ... 'Never cook with it, either.'

Not stopping at French food, the work offered 'Five Courses for Confucius': fried rice (with advice on how to boil rice without making glue), chicken and almonds, sweet-and-sour pork, sweet-and-sour fish, and spring rolls. The book is dated now, but in its time it was a trendsetter. And others in the same vein followed: *Oh For a Man Who Cooks* (1957), *Cooking for Bachelors* (1959) and *Cooking for Brides* (1965).

There was now no longer any excuse for seriously dull cookery books. Nor shortage of light-hearted ones: *Survival in the Doghouse* (John O'Grady, 1973), *The Naked Gourmet* (Hilarie Lindsay and Paul Delprat, 1979) and *Hang on to Your Horse's Doovers* (Kerry Cue, 1987) are among the racier titles.

It was not only humour (or even a hint of sex), however, that persuaded people to buy new cookery books. As we have seen, the women's magazines had found their own winning formula for reaching the masses. Namely: offer them possibilities for food that is exciting-but-safe, different-but-easy; do it with recipes that are easy to follow; put in lots of illustrations to prove it; and finally, show them just how good the finished product will be—in large, gloriously sensuous colour pictures.

Food is no longer fuel—food is pleasure.

FOOD WRITERS: COMMUNICATING FOOD AND COOKERY

Australia can boast a large number of successful cookery writers, reflecting our national attraction for cookery books. Most food lovers would have no trouble naming either a favourite cookery book writer, or one whose recipes they have consistently used over a long period.

Many would award the honour to Margaret Fulton: indeed, she is said to be one of the world's most successful cookery writers. Already a household name following 16 years as cookery editor for *Woman's Day* magazine, she produced her first book, *The Margaret Fulton Cookbook* in 1968. The work was an instant best-seller and became the kitchen manual for hundreds of thousands of housewives. For more than 40 years Margaret Fulton's recipe collections moved with the changing times: entertaining in the early 1970s; French, Italian and Chinese cuisine in the early 1980s; then microwave cooking later on. The secret of her success, according to her followers, is that her recipes can always be trusted to work first time—she takes the risk out of cooking. It is not too hard to make the dish look like the picture.

In parallel with such popular figures as Margaret Fulton, Australia's newspapers and magazines have become significant forces in shaping the way Australians think about food and how they approach it. They have developed complex formulae for selling their own products, and generating advertising revenue, by encouraging the purchase of other people's products. The daily newspapers have their weekly food supplements with lively and topical articles on cookery, restaurant dining and lifestyle. There are recipes to try, usually with an emphasis on novelty and fashion. It does not always matter whether many people actually use the recipes—they don't use their cookery books much either—the real purpose may only be to attract and retain the right kinds of readers. Alternatively, the recipes may be there to extend the use of some manufacturer's product. (It is often interesting to note what the common ingredients or processes of the recipes are, and then make comparison with the advertisements placed nearby.)

FOOD WRITING

... if food writers take seriously issues about commercial food, and the standards of commercial food and ... packaged food, they can have a major influence on quality and on Australians' health. —Gay Bilson

(from top)
The indomitable Margaret Fulton, quite possibly the world's biggest-selling cookery book author
Portrait by Greg Barrett
gelatin silver photograph; 37.2 x 29 cm
Peter Weiss Collection; from the Pictorial Collection

And the cover of one of her cardinal works
(Sydney: Paul Hamlyn/Reed Books, 1970)

FOOD AND SEX

Food and sex have of course been linked from time immemorial. One recent literary instance is provided by Linda Jaivin's popular 1995 novel *Eat Me*, which had already sold 27 000 copies in Australia at the time of the following review in the National Library's *Voices* magazine, and was later published in American and German editions.

> *Eat Me* was the first of the recent literary erotic wave ... Jaivin's success has clearly traded on the erotic label. But although the graphic sex in the book places it in the erotic bed, its dominant mode is really comic. Take the opening paragraph:
>
>> She ran her fingers over the fresh figs. Surprising little sacs they were. Funny, dark and wrinkled, yet so exquisite on the tongue. Mother Nature had surely been thinking of Father Nature when she invented figs ...
>
> The comedy is the real source of pleasure in *Eat Me*, reinforced by the unifying emblem of the book: food ... For Jaivin, eating and sex go hand in hand, and there are always comic messages in the meals eaten, and sometimes otherwise consumed. There are the grapes used when Phillipa attempts to imitate one of her fantasies—where four go in, only three come out. There is the Andalusian white soup and its connection to bodily fluids, oral sex and vegans. There is the gourmet pizza stain on frumpy Helen's favourite beige skirt. The comestibles in each case enhance, interpret, undercut or explain the actions of the characters.
>
> —Neil James, 'The Erotogenic Distaff...', *Voices*, winter, 1997

Art, too, has traditionally represented, or been inspired by, foods—from fruit-laden cornucopias, to Andy Warhol's Campbell's Soup cans. Donald Friend's work is another colourful, sensual instance.

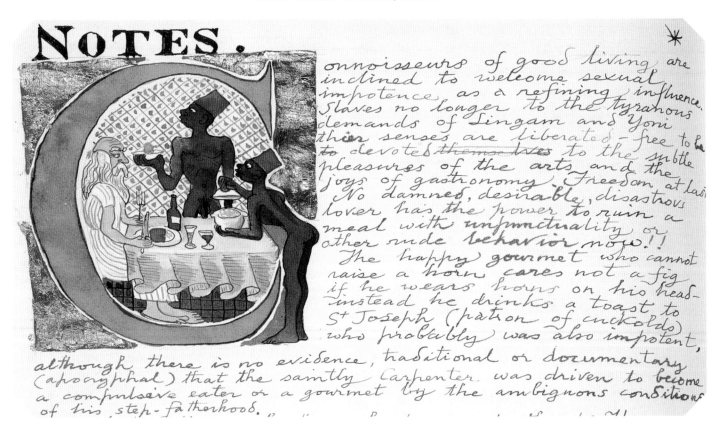

The twentieth century brought increasing opportunities for communicating food and cookery in other ways. Radio broadcasting began in the mid-1920s, and soon cookery experts were giving out recipes over the air. (Slowly, so they could be copied down.) Sometimes there was an accompanying book, as in the case of Bessie Eddy, formerly of the Tasmanian Education Department, and a very early broadcaster on 'attractive cookery' for 3LO Melbourne. Eddy claimed that 'instead of being regarded as a servile duty, cookery is now exalted into a science'. (An interesting feature of her little book was the use of the headings 'matter' and 'method' instead of the more familiar 'ingredients' and 'method'.)

The long-awaited arrival of television in Australia brought with it a new challenge to the nation's eating habits. The evening meal—whether dinner or 'tea'—now became an interruption. There seemed to be three solutions. 1—Turn off the television and eat in peace. (This was unpopular). 2—Move the television into the dining room or kitchen. (This was inconvenient.) Or 3—Keep watching, and eat off your lap. Folklore has it that many preferred option 3. What this did to the appreciation of food can only be imagined. Perhaps it was one of the factors which kept Australia's culinary reputation poor, long after Ted Moloney and the Society of Gourmets had determined to improve it. But the temptation to simplify meals for easy consumption in front of television, or to reduce the amount of time spent in the kitchen preparing them, posed no threat to the food industry, which was quick to respond with the portion-controlled TV dinner—just pop it in the oven to heat, then eat straight from the foil tray. (Saves washing up, too!)

Television also brought new advertising opportunities for food manufacturers. Despite its higher cost, it was an ideal medium for communicating cookery. Now it was possible to show people exactly how a dish was made. The 'Galloping Gourmet' Graham Kerr led a parade of TV cooks across our screens: in the space of half an hour, home audiences watched him prepare and serve such delicacies as roast pork with spiced peaches, grilled lambs' kidneys, or Pacific pie (which he claimed was 'a great deal better' than the Italian pizza it imitated).

An important ingredient in Graham Kerr's success was his infectious enthusiasm. While people may have listened to radio broadcasts to get the recipes or to pick up a few hints, with television cookery programs it was different. True, one could still hope to learn how to make new dishes or improve one's kitchen skills—indeed in the decades that followed Kerr, television opened up to Australians the whole *world* of cookery, to the point that it is hard now to think of a region, foodstuff or technique that has not been presented. But whether one cooked or not, there was a fundamental fascination in watching a lively personality romp around the kitchen with a serious chef's knife in one hand and a glass of wine in the other to produce, with magically little effort, a meal fit for a gourmet. The TV chef had arrived.

And somewhere along the line, 'cookery' became 'entertainment'. As increasing numbers of Australians now do less real cooking for themselves—relying increasingly on 'instant' meals from the supermarket, fast food from takeaways and 'meals out' at cafés and restaurants—more people than ever buy cookery books they never cook from, and watch television demonstrations of dishes they will never make.

LAMBS' KIDNEYS OTAKI

A suitable snack for Sunday night around the fire.

Prepare 4 lambs' kidneys as per basic method (i.e. peel back skin and detach, cut out heavy white ligament); push wooden spikes through each 'wing' to keep flat; broil on cut side for 3 minutes only. Halve four large, firm tomatoes and season with pepper and garlic salt. Place on rack with kidneys round-side uppermost, on top of tomatoes. Brush with butter and finish broiling for three minutes. Fry 4 bacon slices. Take skewer out of kidneys, top them with 4 tablespoons parsley butter, and serve with fried bacon.

—The Graham Kerr Cookbook

Thousands of Australians watched the irrepressible Graham Kerr cavort in front of television cameras, then went out and bought his cookbooks, such as this 1971 British edition of an earlier Australian one. The arrival of colour transmission added to the appeal of such programs
(London: W.H. Allen & Co. (UK), 1971)

CELEBRATING FOOD; THE COOK AS HERO

About the time that cookery books shook off their drabness, grew larger pages and abandoned themselves to riotous displays of colour, the dull business of cookery gave way, as far as many people were concerned, to a popular culture of food. It was not that we became a nation of gastronomes, but simply that we were able to rejoice in abundance. The enjoyment of food—both for itself and as a natural setting for pleasurable social occasions—was no longer the exclusive privilege of the wealthy.

Accompanying this development has been a dramatic resurgence in the concept of the celebrity chef. Though of course celebrated chefs have been around for a long time: one of Australia's first was Hannah Maclurcan, who began her career at the Club Hotel in Toowoomba in the late nineteenth century, subsequently moving to Sydney's Wentworth Hotel in 1901 to make it one of the city's great hotels. Her famous work (*Mrs Maclurcan's Cookery Book*, from 1898) remained in print, in its many editions, for more than 30 years. Much more recent cooking personalities include Ian Parmenter, Gabriel Gaté, Charmaine Solomon and Stephanie Alexander.

(top) The Wentworth Hotel, run at one time by Hannah MacLurcan
From the *Sydney Mail*, 15 December 1920
From the Pictorial Collection

(above) Ian Parmenter's *Consuming Passions* showed how eating well can combine with good health and a modern lifestyle
(Sydney: National Heart Foundation of Australia, 1992)

(right) Stephanie Alexander, famous for good food and good food writing. Author of, among other works, the lavish, brick-sized, best-selling tome *The Cook's Companion* (1996)
Photograph by Greg Barrett
gelatin silver photograph; 37.7 x 28.7 cm
Peter Weiss Collection; from the Pictorial Collection

Australian historians have largely ignored eating, except to mention the privations of the early years and a few significant events since then, or perhaps to offer a generalisation or two. They have taken their lead from the times. Until the early twentieth century (and then only in the women's columns), food—except as an article of production, commerce or public health—was not a subject for public discussion. Yet the issue of Australian foods—how Australians have eaten, and how they continue to eat—is one of the characteristics that define us. Only in the last two decades have scholars and writers begun to fill the void.

The first to trace out a history of Australian cookery since the permanent arrival of Europeans was Anne Gollan, in *The Tradition of Australian Cooking* (1978). Gollan found three overlapping stages of development mirrored in our kitchens. First there was the 'outdoor kitchen', dominating the age of survival and discovery from 1788 to about 1870. Then came the 'outhouse kitchen', symbolising an age of growing awareness and refinement, and lasting roughly from 1850 to 1920. This gave way to the new age of convenience and commercialism, which Gollan called the 'respectable kitchen'.

Michael Symons, writing several years later (*One Continuous Picnic: A History of Eating in Australia*, 1982), also found three developmental stages, and used them to describe a process by which he said Australians became alienated from the sources of their food. First (from 1788 to the 1860s) the growing of food, animals and plants was industrialised by modern methods of production based on specialisation and economies of scale. In terms of feeding, this was the age of bush rations; the dominant form of transport was the sailing ship. The second stage (to the 1930s) saw the industrialisation of the processing and retailing of food, as mass systems of transport, storage and distribution developed to gather, rationalise and sell durable produce to city households and overseas markets. This was the age of tinned and processed food, and of the railways. Third, cooking was industrialised, as factories and restaurants took over most of the work of preparing food for the table. (Anne Gollan's 'respectable kitchen' becoming a small nook for final assembly and dishing-up.) This was the age of convenience foods and of automobiles. In a later book (*The Shared Table: Ideas for Australian Cuisine*, 1993) Symons discussed multiculturalism as the dominant symbol in Australia's modern food and eating culture.

More recently, *A Friend in the Kitchen: Old Australian Cookery Books* (Colin Bannerman, 1996) has examined the books produced around the time of Federation—looking particularly at the kind of food they presented, and why they were written. This work finds that, although the food then was overwhelmingly English in origin and quite recognisably English in style, there was plenty of evidence that colonial cooks had been busy adapting imported traditions to local needs. The process of adaptation was not led by teachers and reformers, but took place in ordinary kitchens in response to the daily realities of availability and storage. The social structure throughout the nineteenth century provided no great refining influence. It was largely an egalitarian food culture. Refinement, when it came, was a product of the romantic movement. It left its mark in the celebration of sweetness, the enrichment of English cookery with novelty and with fanciful names, and the veneration of bush food.

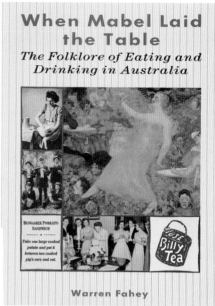

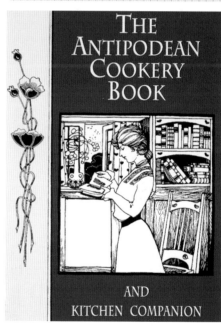

Warren Fahey's *When Mabel Laid the Table: The Folklore of Eating and Drinking in Australia* (1992) is one of a number of new wave food-culture texts
(Sydney: State Library of New South Wales Press, 1992)

The issuing of facsimile editions of such classics as Mina Rawson's 1895 work *The Antipodean Cookery Book and Kitchen Companion* serves a small but enthusiastic market for cookery nostalgia
(Sydney: Kangaroo Press/Simon & Schuster Aust., 1992)

A central approach to defining the distinctive new 'Australian cuisine' is to see it as a blend of Asian with European food and cooking techniques; other commentators have additionally argued the incorporation of traditional 'bush foods'. Among a number of recent books addressing the issue has been Kenneth Leung, Mark Wilson and Carole Ruta's *Fusion: The Watermark Restaurant Cookbook* (Pymble, NSW: HarperCollins, 1997)

In recent years there have also been plenty of books to feed Australians' appetite for cookery nostalgia. Some examples are *A Taste of the Past* (Joyce Allen and Valerie McKenzie, 1977), *When Mabel Laid the Table* (Warren Fahey, 1992), *Grandma's General Store* (Brenda Marshall and Len Moore, 1978), and the *Baby Boomers' Cookbook* (Helen Townsend, 1991). And there has been no shortage of books for the coffee-table. One example, *The 200 Years History of Australian Cooking* (1988, sponsored by the Edgell–Bird's Eye food company) opens with a brief summary of Australian food history, before concentrating on the present, and giving recipes from most of the ethnic groups now represented in Australian society—except, curiously, indigenous Australians.

The WATERMARK Restaurant COOKBOOK

fusion

KENNETH LEUNG
MARK WILSON and CAROLE RUTA

In addition to this, a few of the old cookery books have been reprinted in recent years. Examples from the nineteenth century are Mina Rawson's *Antipodean Cookery Book and Kitchen Companion* from 1895 (republished 1992) and the *Goulburn Cookery Book* from 1899 (republished 1973). Other recent facsimiles are the *Green & Gold Cookery Book* (1960 edition); the *Schauer Cookery Book* (1962 edition) and the *Presbyterian Cookery Book* (1979 edition).

ASIA MEETS BUSH TUCKER?

... if [a distinctive Australian cuisine] has budded ... it is certainly only now in some sort of adolescent phase ... if you agree with me that a cuisine comes out of a peasantry—a regional area cut off from another area, where certain dishes grow up—and this is relevant to Chinese food, as well as to French or Czechoslovakian food ... —then it's far too late ... we're never going to have regionalism in that sort of sense. If you think a cuisine can be defined as something that didn't necessarily come out of regionalism, then it's still going to be a kind of reflective cuisine; it's post-modern, it's self-conscious ...

I sometimes think we're asking [the Asian culinary styles] to suit Australia, we're so excited by it—we're saying: 'Here it is; we're going to make this suit Australia' ... it just seems so utterly stupid not to have taken any notice of it years and years ago ... [but] there's no reason that [the] kind of craft and understanding of extracting flavour from meats and fish [in Escoffier] shouldn't be combined with this new reverence for Asian spices ... —Gay Bilson

THE CONTEMPORARY FOOD DEBATE: FUSION?

Now we are told that we have shaken off the British heritage and that a new Australian food culture has emerged. (Or perhaps is still in process of emerging.) The foodie journalists and leading restaurant chefs have been busy self-consciously defining the 'national cuisine' of the 1990s (for those who wish to have such certainty). The consensus seems to favour some blend of the new-found foods and techniques from Asia with the more familiar customs imported from various parts of Europe. A few advocates have spoken up for 'bush tucker', or some refinement of it. (See feature, opposite page.) And that word 'fresh' keeps popping up.

At the same time, nutritionists tell us that we should improve our diet in the interests of good health: there is a ready market today for books on attractive healthy food—and there probably always will be, for the more health-conscious we become, the more new hazards are discovered.

Recent food history suggests that it is producers, processors and retailers who will have the loudest voice in the ongoing food debate—and that consumers will listen, as long as the former speak of food that is exciting but safe, different but easy, and attractively packaged but cheap. More than ever before, 'freshness', it seems, comes in a packet. And of course all this food is 'healthy'.

The truth is that there never was a single Australian food culture, and probably never will be. Gourmet cookery, as taught in the more expensive books and 'showcased' in the finest restaurants, sets the high fashion. The magazines translate it into popular fashion. Health experts tell us what is good for us. And industry promises healthy, gourmet, convenient food on a budget. Others argue that a true cuisine of the people is one that serves the needs of modern day-to-day living, keeps alive the heritage of newcomers to Australia, and celebrates the traditions of its ancient peoples.

But as far as many are concerned, the real food culture has little to do with ideals and public debate. It is the cookery of ordinary households, as practised in suburban kitchens on ordinary weeknights, after a tiring day at work. And maybe some Australians are still simply content with food-as-fuel.

REVAMPING BUSH TUCKER

Acting parallel with the strong Asian influence on recent Australian cookery has been an increasing interest in use of native Australian foods. An instance of the culinary possibilities is provided by Allan Vousden's 'Kullanteenee Bush Tucker and Promotion', a travelling indigenous culture, educational and catering firm. (The name is modified from 'kullateenee', an Aboriginal word for 'gathering bush food by fire'.)

After serving an apprenticeship at a French restaurant in Sydney, Vousden graduated from East Sydney Food College and went on to cook for oil and mining crews in the Kimberleys, Great Sandy Dessert, Nullarbor Plains and Arnhem Land, where he had contact with local hunter-and-gatherer communities. A member of the Tharawal community of the Campbelltown area in Sydney's south west, he has cooked onstage with Bernard King, and in recent years taken his traditional and revamped Aboriginal cuisine to numerous cultural and food festivals.

Kullanteenee's ingredients come from wide-flung regions of the country: emu meat from South Australia, crocodile from the Northern Territory, boab nuts from Western Australia and witjuti grubs from Central Australia. As Vousden expresses it, 'Aborigines have been cooking great takeaway for thousands of years'.

His menus (with names like 'Seafood Dreaming' and 'Walkabout Buffet') also incorporate such items or ingredients as magpie geese, camel, witjuti grub dip, barramundi-and-yabbie meat crepes, fresh garden salad with macadamia nuts, and rosella-flower fruit (native hibiscus) biscuits. For refreshment there is Kakadu plum cordial, or wattle-seed drink ('similar to coffee but no caffeine'). And for sweets, a bush pavlova ('succulent bush fruits and berries coated with wattle cream') or drop cakes (described as 'traditional Koori pancakes, served with bush fruits and cream').

BUSH TUCKER

AUSTRALIA'S WILD FOOD HARVEST

TIM LOW

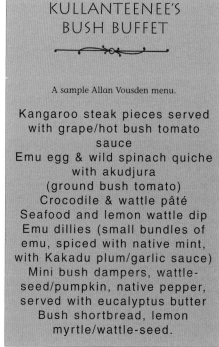

KULLANTEENEE'S
BUSH BUFFET

A sample Allan Vousden menu.

Kangaroo steak pieces served with grape/hot bush tomato sauce
Emu egg & wild spinach quiche with akudjura (ground bush tomato)
Crocodile & wattle pâté
Seafood and lemon wattle dip
Emu dillies (small bundles of emu, spiced with native mint, with Kakadu plum/garlic sauce)
Mini bush dampers, wattle-seed/pumpkin, native pepper, served with eucalyptus butter
Bush shortbread, lemon myrtle/wattle-seed.

(top) title page of *Bush Tucker: Australia's Wild Food Harvest*, which explored Australian native foods (North Ryde, NSW: Angus & Robertson/HarperCollins, 1989)

(left) Koori chef Allan Vousden's crocodile-and-wattle pâté and spicy bush dips

DRINKS OF THE GODS

Eric Rolls

Water came first (and whoever brewed water was a pastmaster), then came beer, then wine, both greeted so joyously by the ancients that they invented Bacchus to explain them. Who else but a god could create such wonders?

BEER

Since he had no hops, John Boston, who made the first beer in Sydney in 1796 from maize 'properly malted', used Cape Gooseberries to counter sweetness and control unwanted yeasts and bacteria. Later brewers made use of Broad-leaf Hopbush (*Dodonaea viscosa*). Then in 1822 W. Shoobridge, who had grown hops in England, planted setts in a valley near Hobart Town. Hop growing became an important Tasmanian industry. For more than 100 years up to 3000 pickers on ladders or stilts brought in a careful harvest from the vines on tall trellises.

Good beer is a living thing. It is not filtered, not pasteurised, there is sufficient residual sugar left in the bottles for yeasts to feed on. Australia's best beers, outstanding at any level, are made in South Australia by Cooper and Sons: Sparkling Ale and Extra Stout. Both respond to cellaring for at least 18 months. Good beer is worth the consideration of any palate. Only short-lived, fizzy, commercial beers fit the advertisement, 'That didn't touch the sides'.

(right) Eric Rolls
Photograph by Craig Voevodin

(below) Refreshment break at a waterhole in country New South Wales
From the Pictorial Collection

Donald Friend (1914–89)
Bacchanal
From 'Ayam-Ayam Kesayangan'
(Donald Friend Diaries)
From the Manuscript Collection

WINE

No beer, however, carries the complications of wine, an essence exceeded only by the original soup that produced life. Wine contains up to 650 different chemicals and minerals including an unknown number of compounds of sugar known as glycosides that exclude water and bind flavours within them until acids and enzymes break down the case and allow water to wash the flavours out.

The sophistication of early winemaking is startling. By the first century AD, already building on the experience of 3000 years, Roman winemakers were sending vine dressers into the vineyards to snip off leaves and allow sunlight to ripen the bunches. They matured the wine in underground cellars, excluding contaminants such as leather, cheese, figs and old casks as though they knew there were wild yeasts and bacteria on them. They regarded 25 years maturation as a short period—the best wines were put down for 200 years.

By the time the first grapes came to Australia the English had developed a liking for wine, especially the port wine fortified by brandy while it was still sweet by English companies which had set up in Portugal. But like the passengers and the livestock, the grape cuttings had a difficult passage.

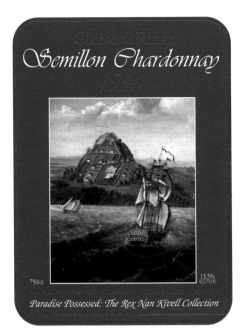

(from top)
Innumerable societies and community organisations have produced their own cookery books or labelled wines as fundraisers. This label, organised by the Friends of the National Library of Australia, celebrates the exhibition *Paradise Possessed: The Rex Nan Kivell Collection* 1998–99

An early Australian wines promotion booklet (Adelaide: Australian Wine Overseas Marketing Board, c.1930)

As Arthur Bowes Smyth, surgeon on *Lady Penrhyn* of the First Fleet reported, during a heavy storm after leaving the Cape of Good Hope:

> the Tubs in the Cabin wt. the Banana plants, Grape Vines &ca. Broke from their fastenings & were thrown out of the tubs & much hurt.

Despite the catastrophe, when planted next to Governor Phillip's portable canvas house on the south-east shore of Sydney Cove (near the present Museum of Sydney), the grapes grew so well that Phillip wrote in his journal:

> The wines of New South Wales may perhaps here after be sought with civility and become an indispensable part of the luxury of European tables.

Anthracnose, a necrotic disease carried by Coast Wattle (*Acacia sophorae*), attacked those first grapes, but not before they yielded some good bunches and 8000 cuttings for a government farm on the south bank of the river at Parramatta, and 900 for Phillip Schaeffer, a German settler who was granted 140 acres (56 hectares) on the north bank of the river. Schaeffer was our first private vigneron.

In 1816 Gregory Blaxland, famous for his crossing of the Blue Mountains, began planting on his beautiful 'Brush Farm' in the present Dundas Valley–Eastwood area of Sydney, with South African varieties resistant to anthracnose. Two hogsheads (477 litres) that he took to England in 1827 earned him a gold medal from The Royal Society of Arts in London, whose members found the wine 'wholly free from the earthy flavour which unhappily characterises most of the Cape wines'. (If he had had the same faith in his wine as the Roman makers, he might have put a few hogsheads into a cellar dug into the Blue Mountains, saying 'This will be ready for the year 2000 celebrations'.)

John Macarthur also played a pioneering role in our winemaking history. Exiled after one of his more violent quarrels, he spent the years 1815 and 1816 walking Europe with his sons James and William, collecting cuttings 'from the most celebrated vineyards of Burgundy, Champagne, Dauphine and Longuedoc'. The Macarthurs planted the first vineyard at Camden in 1820. In 1827, as the first commercial producers in Australia, they made 90 000 litres of wine, equal to 10 000 cases of today's bottles—the 1990s output of such wineries as Cape Mentelle on the Margaret River (Western Australia), or Huntington Estate at Mudgee (New South Wales).

In 1825 James Busby, strangely unhappy despite his knowledge of wine and viticulture, made an important planting of vines in the Hunter Valley of New South Wales. Then, after travelling the vineyards of France and Spain in 1832, he brought back 500 cuttings that still influence Australian wine, since Shiraz and Chardonnay (until the 1960s known as White Pinot) were among them.

Names still associated with Australian wines became known in the 1830s: George Wyndham and Dr Henry John Lindeman in the Hunter Valley, and John Reynell and Richard Hamilton in South Australia. Although they could make good wine, winemakers had prejudice and inexperienced palates to cope with. When 100 young Swiss winemakers came to Victoria and planted near Geelong in the early 1840s and found they could not sell their table wine, they fortified it and thus prospered during the gold rush. Even the later wines of Dr Christopher Rawson Penfold did not appear on top tables in the colonies. Anybody earning more than £500 a year was obliged by snobbery to serve imported wine.

Beer didn't keep very well on board, so only a month's supply was victualled to the Endeavour. (A common remedy for spoilt beer was to add some flour, sugar and salt and place it before the galley fire.) Beer-making processes were rather haphazard at the time and the beer would probably have been water in which hops were floated— giving a small alcohol content of 2–5 per cent. Sailors were known to strengthen this with rum or brandy, making a potent brew called 'flip'.

When beer supplies were exhausted they were replaced with wine. The Endeavour's *wine was bought primarily in Madeira, and placed in 42 empty gauged barrels carried from Plymouth for that purpose. Wine was drunk unaged, and spoiled rapidly because corks were not in use at the time. Sailors usually preferred beer over wine.*

When both beer and wine had been exhausted, sailors were served 'the sailor's sheet anchor' rum. From around 1740, rum was mixed with water and called 'grog' (from Admiral Vernon's nickname, Old Grogram, bestowed from the material from which his cloak was made). This helped to prevent the disciplinary problems that occurred due to drunkenness. The amount of water used was left to the discretion of the captain and depended on the climate and on the quality of the water. Cook's daily ration of slightly more than a quarter of a litre of rum was mixed with water to total a litre of grog. It would have been about 18 per cent alcohol by volume (comparable to a modern aperitif). Drinking hoarded grog offered a few hours of oblivion to sailors, helping pass away the time. It also had a pleasantly warming effect in cold climates, and its sharp taste relieved the monotonous ship diet.

—from CD-ROM Endeavour:
Captain Cook's Journal 1768–71

(top left) Celebrated winemaker Wolf Blass
Photograph by Greg Barrett
gelatin silver photograph; 37.5 x 29.6 cm
Peter Weiss Collection; from the Pictorial Collection

(top right) Endeavour *replica*

Maurice O'Shea, who was still making superb red wine in the Hunter Valley in the 1950s, was known to few people. It was considered unmanly to drink wine, not even beer was allowed in hotel dining rooms. The general attitude, enforced by law, was 'This here's for drinkin', that there's for eatin''. It was well into the 1960s before wine became socially acceptable. By then Australia's greatest vines had chosen their districts: Shiraz (called Hermitage) and Semillon (called Riesling) in the Hunter Valley; Riesling (called Rhine Riesling) in the Clare Valley of South Australia; and Muscadelle and Red Frontignac had chosen Rutherglen in northern Victoria, where Chambers, Morris and Baileys make liqueur Tokay and Muscat famous throughout the world.

Chardonnay has since joined Australia's strengths and it has adopted many areas, making a different wine in each district. Great modern makers like Max Schubert, Brian Croser, Dr John Middleton, Peter Lehmann and Dr Andrew Pirie have established a standard from which any wine can be judged. And many younger vignerons are now making great wines. Other districts and other grapes are being proved.

Wine is a healthy drink, but that would be a perverse reason for drinking it: the real wonder of wine is that it brings so much extra richness to life, while increasing the years in which to enjoy it.

BIBLIOGRAPHY

Most of the publications listed below have appeared more than once, either as revised editions or reprints. First editions are not available for all the earlier works. However, in order to give an indication of the place of each text in the time sequence, only the initial publication date (whether exact or approximate) has been given. Since nearly all items were published in Australia, details of publisher and place have generally been omitted. Items which have a general or collective author, or which are better known by a popular title rather than their author, are also entered by their title.

Abbott, Edward ('an Australian Aristologist') *The English and Australian Cookery Book: Cookery for the Many, as Well as for the 'Upper Ten Thousand'*. London, 1864.

Allen, Joyce; McKenzie, Valerie *A Taste of the Past: Early Australian Cooking*. 1977.

Alsop, Patricia J. *Readership in Victoria, c.1835–1865: With Particular Emphasis on Mrs Annie (Baxter) Dawbin as a Representative Reader*. Bibliographical Society of Australia and New Zealand Bulletin vol. 17 no. 1, 1993.

Aronson, Zara *XXth Century Cooking and Home Decoration*. 1900.

[*Australian Woman's Mirror*] *The Woman's Mirror Cookery Book: A Selection of 2,000 Recipes from the Australian Woman's Mirror*. 1937.

Australian Women's Weekly, The. [Magazine. Australian Consolidated Press. From 1933 onwards.]

[——] *Cookery for Parties*. n.d.

—— *Family Dinners*. n.d.

Baldwin, Nancy *Dollar Cook Book*. 196–.

Bannerman, Colin *A Friend in the Kitchen: Old Australian Cookery Books*. 1996.

Barossa Cookery Book, The: see 'Soldiers' Memorial Institute'.

Barton, Ruth *Household Technology in Western Australia 1900–1950*. In *Oral History Association of Australia Journal* no. 7.

[Beeton, Isabella] *Mrs Beeton's Cookery Book and Household Guide*. London, 1892.

Beeton, Isabella *The Book of Household Management*. London, 1861 (facsimile London, 1982).

Bryden-Brown, John *Ads That Made Australia: How Advertising Has Shaped Our History and Lifestyle*. 1981.

Burgmann, Verity; Lee, Jenny (eds) *Constructing a Culture*. 1988.

Cannon, Michael *Life in the Cities* (vol. 3 of *Australia in the Victorian Age*). 1975.

Chong, Elizabeth *The First Happiness: Chinese Cooking for Australia*. 1982.

Clark, C.M.H. *A History of Australia* (vol. 1). 1962 (1978).

[Commonwealth Rationing Commission; Department of Health] *Planning Meat Ration Meals*. n.d; c.1943.

[Contributors] *Green and Gold Cookery Book*. 1924.

[Contributors] *Something Different for Dinner*. 1936.

Cooking Better Electrically: A Complete Guide to Modern Electric Cooking …: see State Electricity Commission of Victoria.

[Cosmopolitan Publishing Co.] *First Australian Continental Cookery Book*. 193–.

Country Women's Association (Bundaberg Branch) *CWA Cookery Book*. 1928.

—— (Esk Valley, Tasmania) *The Esk Valley Cookery Book*. n.d.

—— (New South Wales) *Calendar of Puddings: A Recipe for Each Day of the Year*. 1931.

—— (New South Wales) *The Coronation Cookery Book*. 1937.

—— (South Australia) *Calendar of Meat and Fish Recipes: One for Every Day in the Year*. 1956.

—— (Western Australia) *The CWA Cookery Book and Household Hints*. 1936.

Cue, Kerry *Hang on to Your Horse's Doovers*. 1987.

Donovan, Maria Kozslik *Continental Cookery in Australia*. 1955.

Drake, Lucy *Everylady's Cook Book*. 1923; later editions revised by Dorothy M. Giles.

Drummond, J.C. and Wilbraham, Anne *The Englishman's Food: Five Centuries of English Diet*. London, 1939 (republished London, 1991).

Dunne, Sarah *Wartime Cookery*. 1945.

Eddy, Bessie *Bessie Eddy Cookery Book*. c.1935.

[Education Department, Melbourne] *Cookery the Australian Way*. 1966.

Ewers, Dora *The History of Home Economics in New South Wales Schools*. In *Journal of the Home Economics Association of Australia*, vol. 1 no. 1, May 1969.

Fahey, Warren *When Mabel Laid the Table: The Folklore of Eating and Drinking in Australia*. 1992.

[*First Australian Continental Cookery Book*: see 'Cosmopolitan Publishing Co.']

Floate, Dorothy *Mrs Dorothy Floate's 'Secret of Success' Cookery Book*. 1985.

—— *Mrs Floate's 'Secret of Success' Cookery Book*, vol. 1 (cakes—pastries—biscuits) n.d; vol. 2 (meats—vegetables—puddings) 1950; vol. 3 (preserves) 1947.

Frost, Alan *Botany Bay Mirages: Illusions of Australia's Convict Beginnings*, Melbourne University Press, 1994.

Fulton, Margaret (cookery editor) *Campbell's Treasury of Recipes: 530 Wonderful 'Cooking with Soup' Recipes*. n.d.

Fulton, Margaret *Margaret Fulton Cookbook*. 1968.

Futter, Emily *Australian Home Cookery*. 1923.

Geechoun, Roy *Cooking the Chinese Way*. 1948.

Gelencser, Janos *The Continental Flavour*. c.1950s.

Gilmore, Mary (ed.) *The Worker Cook Book*. 1915.

Glasse, Hannah ('by a lady') *The Art of Cookery Made Plain and Easy*. London, 1747 (facsimile London, 1983).

Gollan, Anne *The Tradition of Australian Cooking*. 1978.

Goode, John *The World Guide to Cooking with Fruit & Vegetables*. 1973.

[*Goulburn Cookery Book, The*: see Rutledge, Mrs Forster (Jean)]

[*Green and Gold Cookery Book*: see 'Contributors']

Hackett, (Lady) Deborah (ed.) *The Australian Household Guide*. 1916.

Hayes, Babette *Barbecue Cooking*. 1970.

Home Economics Teachers' Group, Melbourne *Approach to Cookery: An Elementary Cookery Book for Post Primary Schools*. 1962.

Hutchinson, R.C. *Food for the People of Australia*. 1957.

[Ideal Home Library] *Australian Home Cookery: 850 Tested Recipes and Practical Hints on Marketing*. c.1935.

Kerr, Graham *Entertaining with Kerr*. 1966.

—— *The Graham Kerr Cookbook*. 1966.

King, Annie *Carry On Cookery Book*. 1951 (10th edition).

Kingston, Beverley *My Wife, My Daughter and Poor Mary Anne*. 1975.

[*Kingswood Cookery Book, The*: see Wicken, Harriet]

Kyle, Noeline *Her Natural Destiny: The Education of Women in New South Wales*. 1986.

Lady Victoria Buxton Girls' Club, Adelaide, South Australia *The Kookaburra Cookery Book of Culinary and Household Recipes and Hints*. c.1911.

[*Leader, The*] *The Leader Spare Corner Book*. Nos 1–2–3 1931; Nos 4–5–6 1934.

Lindsay, Hilarie (text); Delprat, Paul (illustrations) *The Naked Gourmet*. 1979.

Lo, Kenneth *Chinese Food*. 1972.

Ludlow, Eugenie P. *Gas Cookery*. 1939.

McGowan, Henrietta C. *The Keeyuga Cookery Book*. 1911.

McKenzie, F. Violet (for the Electrical Association for Women) *Cookery Book and Electrical Guide*. c.1936.

Maclurcan, Hannah *Mrs Maclurcan's Cookery Book*. 1898.

Mallos, Tess; Argyriou, Ellen (for Edgell–Birds Eye) *The 200 Years History of Australian Cooking*. 1988.

Marshall, Brenda; Moore, Len *Grandma's General Store*. 1978.

Meredith, Louisa (Mrs Charles) *Notes and Sketches of New South Wales*. 1844 (facsimile 1973).

—— *My Home in Tasmania ...* 1852 (facsimile edition, Griffin Press, 1979).

Methodist Central Mission (Hobart) *Hobart Cookery Book of Tested Recipes, Household Hints and Home Remedies*. n.d.

Michell, Alexandra *Particular Picnics*. 1985.

Moloney, Ted; Molnar, George (drawings). *Cooking for Bachelors*. 1959.

—— *Cooking for Brides*. 1965.

Moloney, Ted; Coleman, Deke; Molnar, George (drawings) *Oh, for a French Wife!* 1952.

Moloney, Ted *Ted Moloney's Easy Gourmet Cookbook*. 1978.

Mundy, Godfrey Charles *Our Antipodes: Or Residence and Rambles in the Australasian Colonies*. (3 vols.) London, 1852 (3rd edition).

Muskett, Philip E. (Dr) *The Art of Living in Australia*. 1893 (facsimile 1987) (see also entries for Wicken, Harriet).

National Library of Australia–Australian National Maritime Museum *Endeavour: Captain Cook's Journal 1768–71* (CD-ROM), 1998.

Newman, Lilian (for SAGASCO) *Better Cooking ... by Gas*. 1959.

NSW Public School Cookery Teachers Association *Common-Sense Cookery Book*. 1914.

O'Grady, John *Survival in the Doghouse*. 1973.

Oxley, Deborah *Convict Maids: The Forced Migration of Women to Australia*, Melbourne University Press, 1996.

Peacock, Jean I. *A History of Home Economics in New South Wales*. 1982.

Periam, (Hon.) Jonathan *The Pictorial Home and Farm Manual ... Adapted to the Australasian Colonies*. 1885.

[*Planning Meat Ration Meals*: see 'Commonwealth Rationing Commission']

Porter, John D. *The Chef Suggests: Strange and Exciting Dishes with Delicacies of the Table*. 1949.

Presbyterian Women's Missionary Association (NSW) *Cookery Book of Good and Tried Receipts*. 1896.

Presbyterian Women's Missionary Union (Queensland) *W.M.U. Cookery Book*. 1894.

Quayle, Eric *Old Cook Books: An Illustrated History*. New York, 1978.

Raffald, Elizabeth *The Experienced English Housekeeper: For the Use and Ease of Ladies, Housekeepers, Cooks &c.* London, 1782 (8th edition; facsimile London, 1970).

Rankin, H. *Principles of Practical Cookery for School Pupils*. c.1905.

Rawson, Mina (Mrs Lance) *The Antipodean Cookery Book and Kitchen Companion*. 1895 (facsimile 1992).

Ross, Isabel *Cookery Class Recipes: As Taught in the Kitchens of the Metropolitan Gas Company*. 1900.

Rutledge, Mrs Forster (Jean) *The Goulburn Cookery Book*. c.1899 (facsimile 1973).

Schauer, A. and M. *The Schauer Cookery Book*. 1909.

Sharman, Annie Louisa *SAGASCO Cookery Book*. c.1931.

Sherington, Geoffrey *Australia's Immigrants 1788–1988*. 1990 (2nd edition).

Smith, E. *The Compleat Housewife: Or, Accomplish'd Gentlewomans Companion*. London, 1753 (15th edition; facsimile London, 1968).

Smith, H. Nora Curle *Thermo-Electrical Cooking Made Easy*. 1907.

Society of Gourmets; Molnar, George (drawings); Coleman, L. *Oh for a Man Who Cooks*. 1957.

[Soldiers' Memorial Institute, Tanunda] *The Barossa Cookery Book*. 1917.

Solomon, Charmaine *Chinese Cooking: Natural Recipes for Healthy Living*. 1982.

[*Something Different for Dinner*: see 'Contributors']

South Australian Advertiser. From 1858.

[State Electricity Commission of Victoria] *Cooking Better Electrically: A Complete Guide to Modern Electric Cooking ...* c.1960s.

[Sun News–Pictorial] *Australian Cookery of Today*. c.1943.

Sydney [Morning] Herald. From 1831.

Sydney Gazette and New South Wales Advertiser. From 1803.

Symons, Michael *One Continuous Picnic: A History of Eating in Australia*. 1982.

—— *The Shared Table: Ideas for Australian Cuisine*. 1993.

Tench, Watkin *A Complete Account of the Settlement at Port Jackson in New South Wales*. London, 1793 (republished 1996).

Townsend, Helen *The Baby Boomers' Cookbook*. 1991.

Twopeny, Richard E.N. *Town Life in Australia*. 1883 (facsimile 1973).

[War Chest Fund] *War Chest Cookery Book*. 1917.

Ward, Russel *The Australian Legend*. 1958 (1978).

West Redfern Cookery School *The Public School Girls' Book of Recipes*. 1908.

Wicken, Harriet (Mrs) *The Kingswood Cookery Book*. 1888; 1898.

—— *Recipes Given by Mrs Wicken at Cookery Class, Warrnambool*. 1888[?].

[See also Muskett, Philip, E. *The Art of Living in Australia*, for which Harriet Wicken compiled the recipes]

Wilkinson, Alfred J. *The Australian Cook: A Complete Manual of Cookery Suitable for the Australian Colonies*. 1876.

Wilson, Trevor (ed.) *Best of the Bake-Off Recipes*. 1969.

Winning, Ella M. *The Household Manual*. 1899.

INDEX